Color by DESIGN

with Linda M. Poole

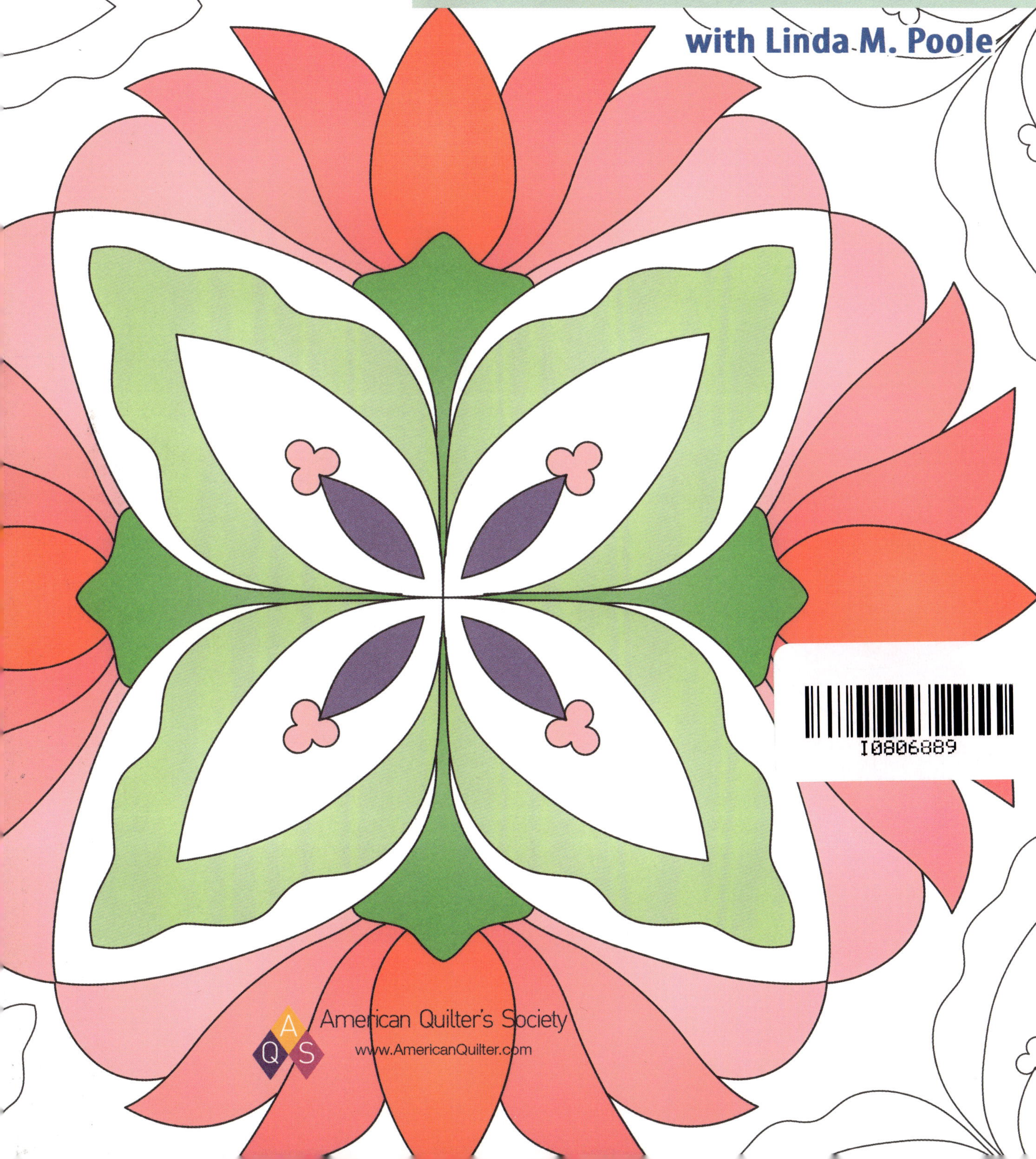

American Quilter's Society
www.AmericanQuilter.com

The American Quilter's Society or AQS is dedicated to quilting excellence. AQS promotes the triumphs of today's quilter, while remaining dedicated to the quilting tradition. We believe in the promotion of this art and craft through AQS Publishing and AQS QuiltWeek®.

Illustrations: Lynda Smith
Graphic Design: Elaine Wilson
Cover Design: Sarah Bozone
Assistant Editor: Adriana Fitch
Director of Publications /Content Editor: Kimberly Holland Tetrev

Additional copies of this book may be ordered from the American Quilter's Society, PO Box 3290, Paducah, KY 42002-3290, or online at www.ShopAQS.com.

American Quilter's Society
www.AmericanQuilter.com

Library of Congress Cataloging-in-Publication Data

Pending

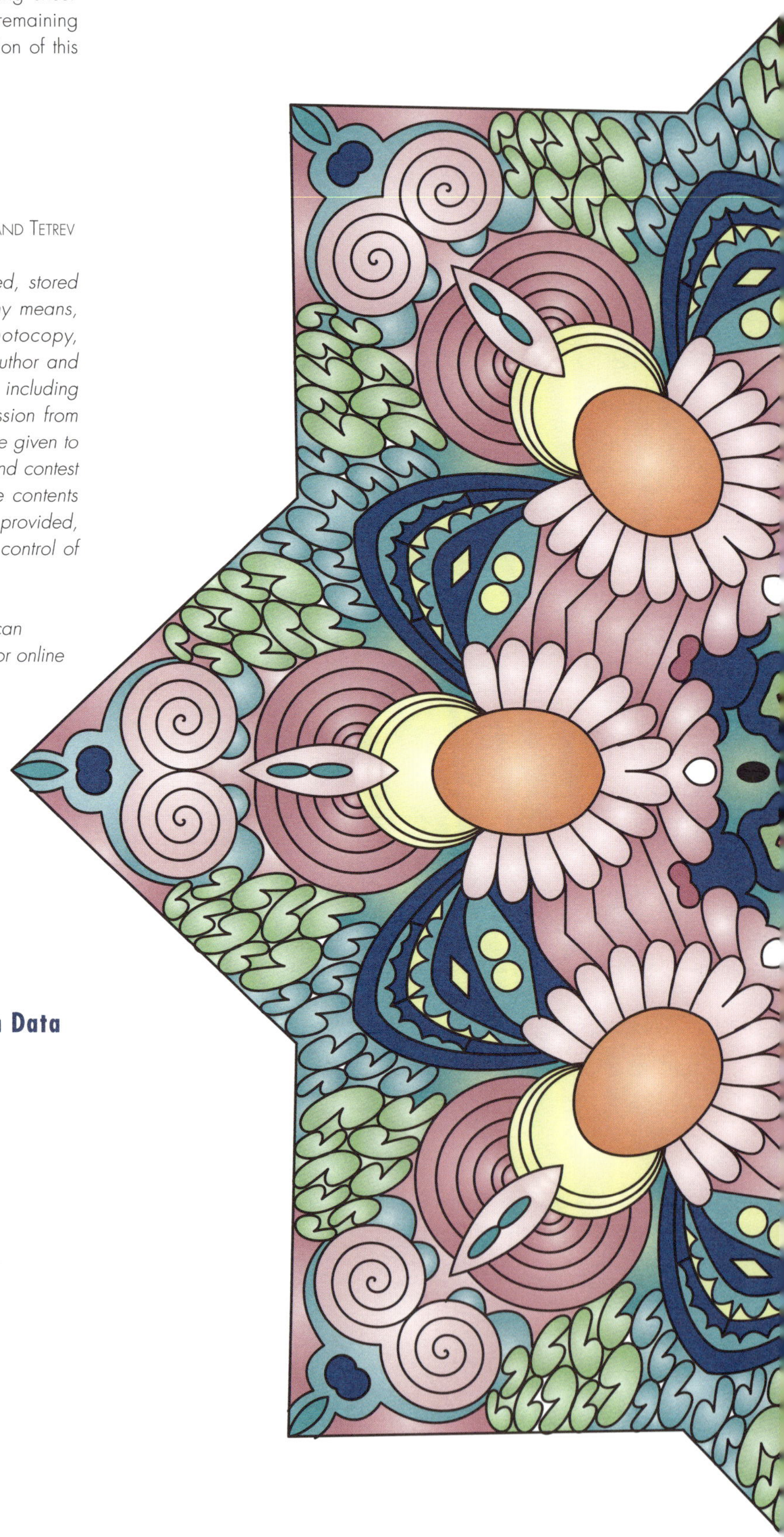

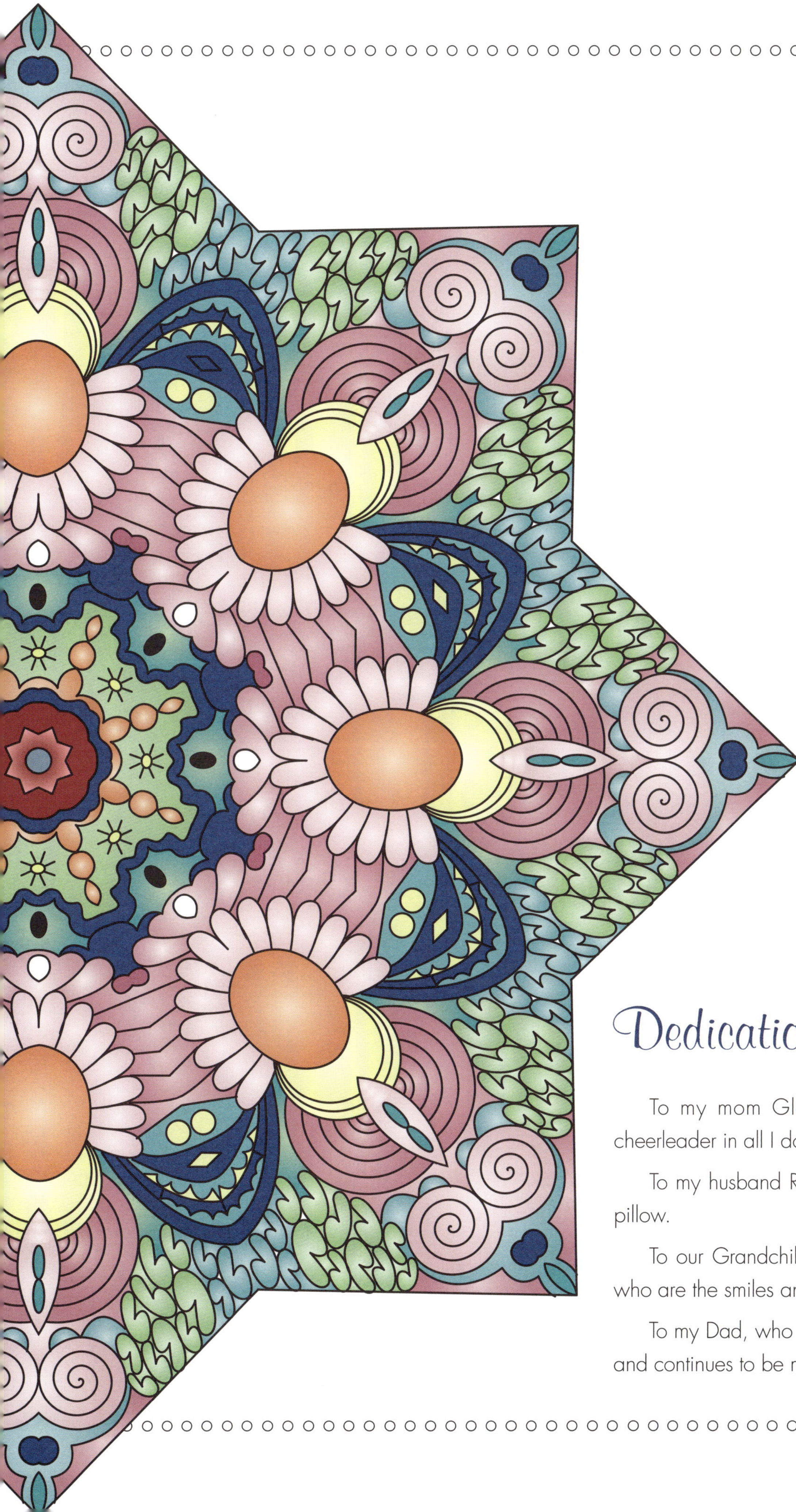

Dedication

To my mom Gloria, who is my constant cheerleader in all I do.

To my husband Ray, who is my rock and my pillow.

To our Grandchildren, Gabriella and Dante, who are the smiles and belly laughs in life.

To my Dad, who watches over me in Heaven and continues to be my muse with wings.

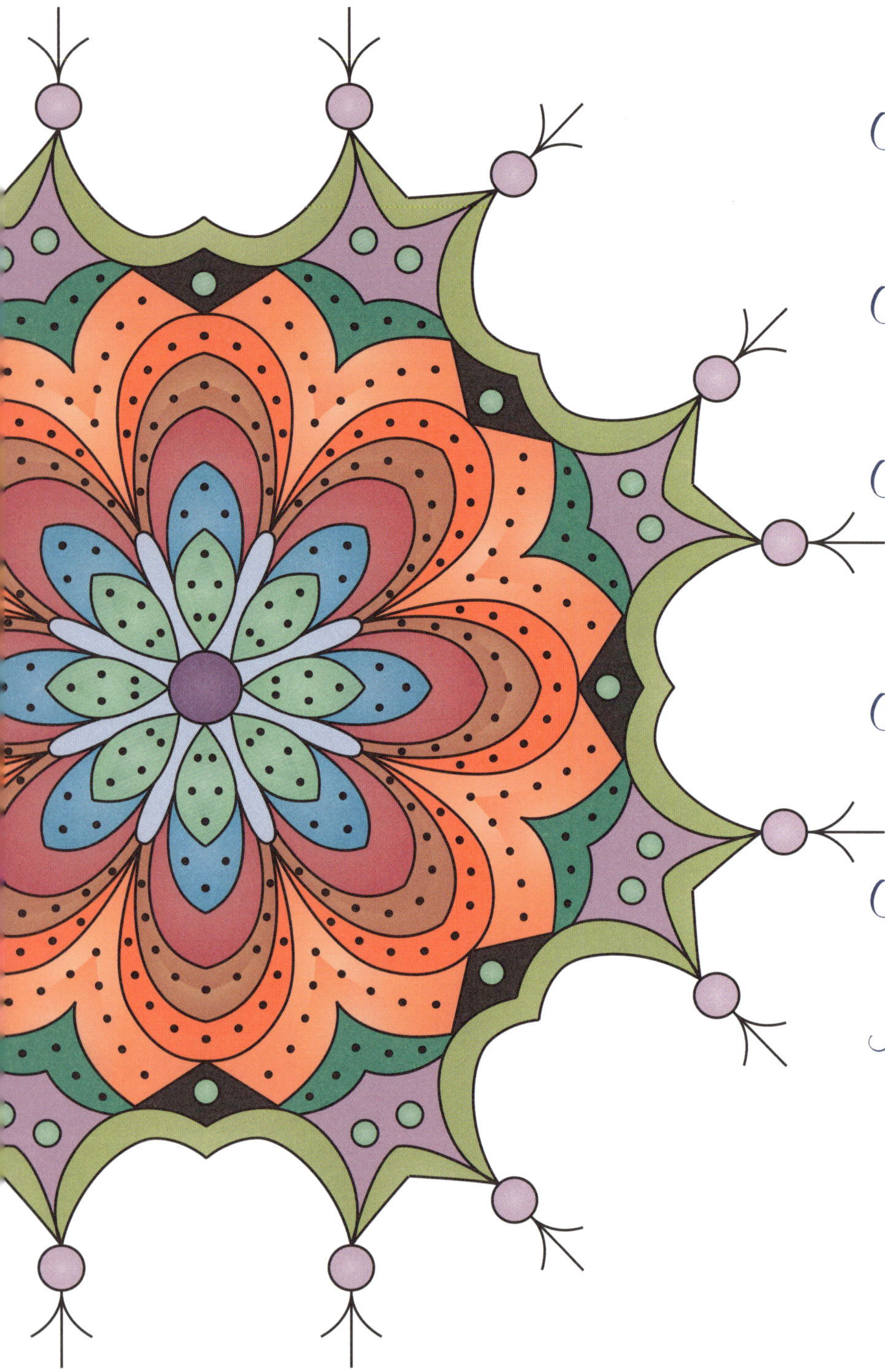

Contents

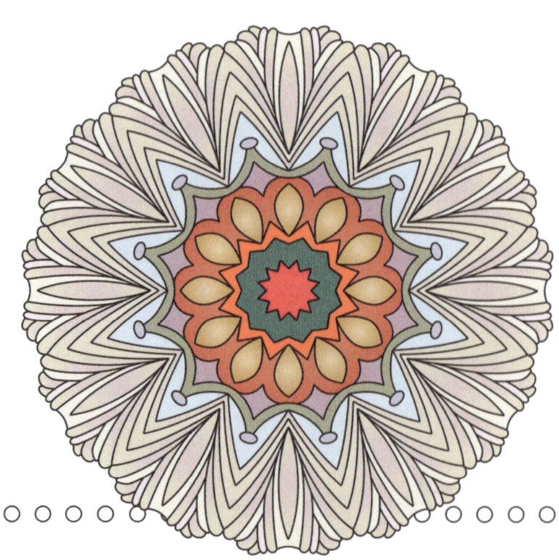

Coloring: What Is It... The Best of Both Worlds

It seems the creative world has gone coloring crazy. Adult coloring books are topping the bestseller book lists and selling by the thousands. The good news is that the only thing crazy about coloring is the number of books and followers the trend has produced. The craft is set for all types. There are no age barriers, nor is there a distinction based on socio-economic factors. The audience is wide, because the level of artistic skill ranges from beginner to advanced. From the Comfortable Shoes Studio blog: *Adult Coloring Books and Art Therapy,* "coloring is an effective tool in reducing agitation, easing anxiety, and helping someone to contain their emotions in the short term." The advantages are clear. It is an art form that not only provides a method for de-stressing, but stimulates the brain. This seemingly simple craft provides the best of both worlds.

The stimulation of the brain allows for areas of creativity to be activated. Once the brain-function is set to create, barring self-consciousness, a flow of activity emerges. Simply put, we stop thinking about what we cannot do and start to color. Before you know it, you have stopped recognizing those thoughts of critical assessment and you are enjoying the moment. This ability to move beyond the demands of life, to enjoy creative expression has found its place in coloring. So much so, that while it has been used as a tool for therapy, it is now becoming mainstream.

The flow of coloring is developed at young ages through the recognition of colors, while children develop fine motor skills and the powerful ability to create world perspective through color. Now the world of coloring has come full circle. Adults are learning the use of coloring to make sense of their worlds, as well.

In addition to its stress relieving properties, coloring has become a social activity. Groups are forming to color together. The dedicated have gone so far as to name themselves colorists. Coloring has even been touted as a means of relaxation to ease into sleep.

Once considered just a children's activity, coloring has evolved as a viable means to explore creativity, provide relaxation, and build socialization.

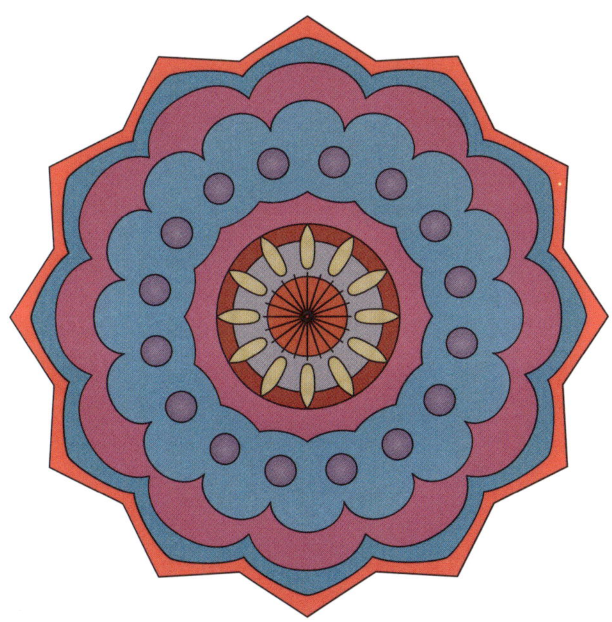

Coloring: How to Do It...Get Ready

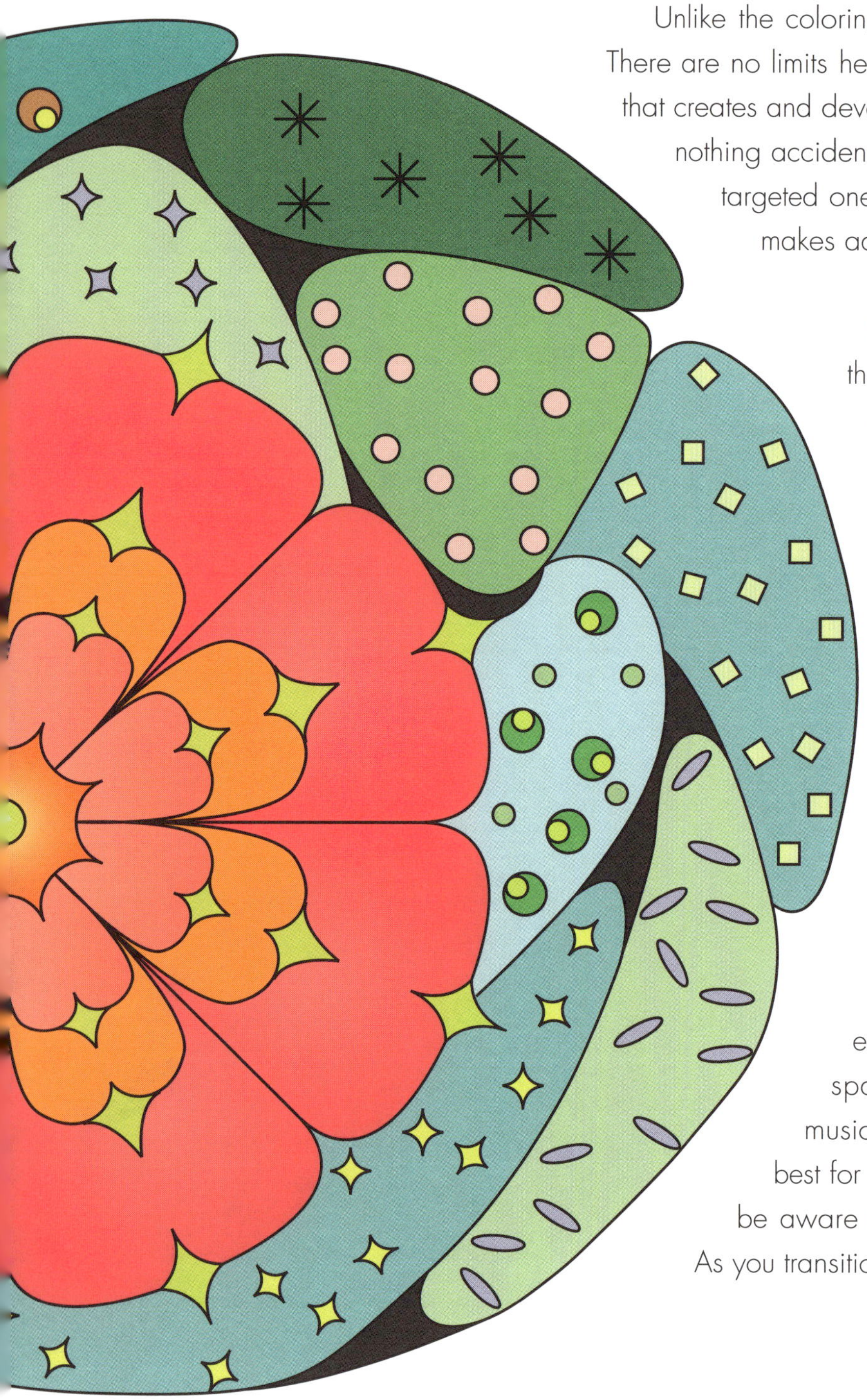

Unlike the coloring rules of our youth, you get to make your own. There are no limits here. It begins with ideation. Ideation is the process that creates and develops new concepts, ideas, and methods. There is nothing accidental about adult coloring. The artistic endeavor is a targeted one. The great number and variety of coloring books makes adult coloring an "on-purpose" activity.

Even with the deliberate attitude toward coloring, there remains an element of serendipity. There is a process of discovery. Gone are the days of strict standards of performance. Although "staying in the lines" is still recommended. This means the approach to coloring must combine discipline, while remaining playful.

To begin your coloring, you may want to go it alone. You will want to find what, when, and where you want to go to color, as you get ready. The answers to all three "w" questions will make a difference in your experience. Do you like large, open spaces or small, closed spaces to color? Do you find you are more alert and energetic in the morning or evening when you color? Do you like bright, quiet spaces or do you like shaded spaces filled with music? The combinations and details for what works best for you are waiting to be uncovered. You should also be aware that creative spaces sometimes require change. As you transition, be aware, and recreate your coloring space.

Coloring: Tools of the Trade...Crayons and Beyond

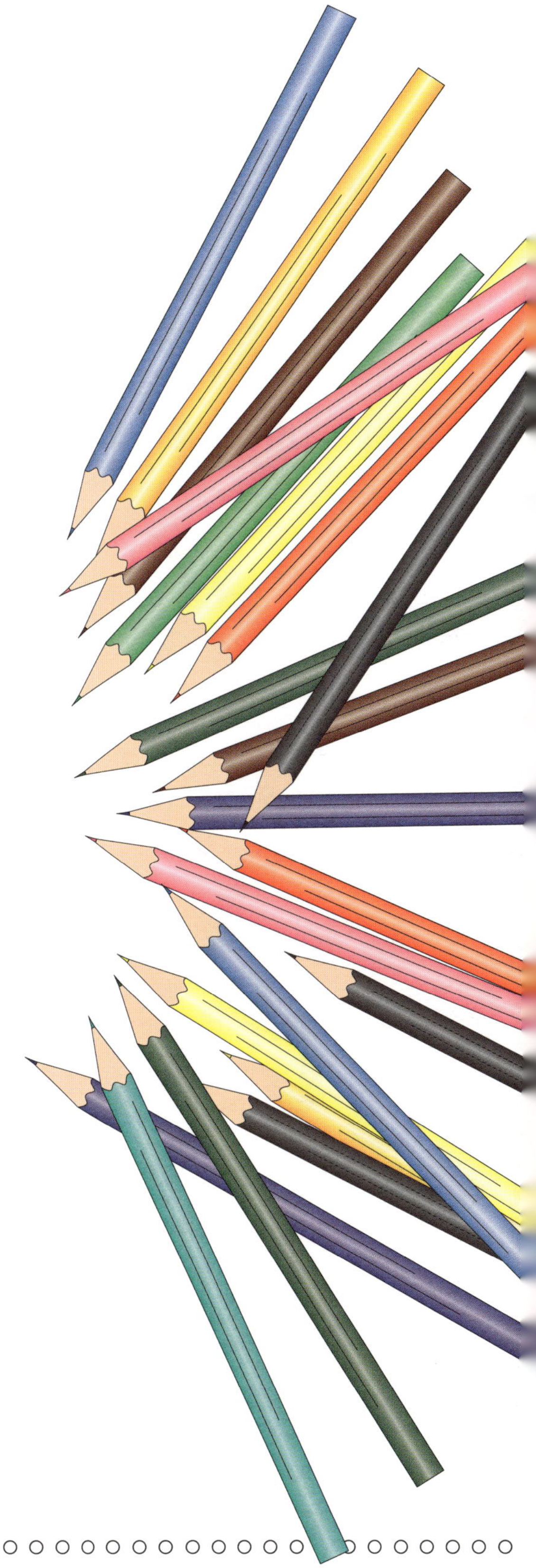

As with anything we create, there are tools that are necessary for our success. It is no different with coloring. There is no shortage of different tools that will allow you to get started and to advance. Overall, the cost to color can advance with your skill, as well. However, coloring is a relatively inexpensive way to "get in touch" with your creative side.

Materials (medium) Overview: These tools come in such a variety it might seem overwhelming, at first glance. Take heart, this just means there is a right tool for you. Some options can be purchased individually, rather than sets. You will find that usual tools fall into four categories: crayons, pencils, markers, and pens. The tools can be mixed and matched to create new colors and textures. The list below is intended to "get you started" and is not meant to be exhaustive.

Crayons are still tried and true. Go ahead and treat yourself to the big box.
Types: Wax, Twistable

Pencils are a staple.
Types: Wax, Watercolor, Tri-tone, Pastel, Vibrant

Markers can be alcohol based, so they may take longer to dry.
Types: Refillable, fine point, Pastel, Bold, Fine Point, Multicultural, Gel

Gel Pens provide opaque color.
Types: Neon, Glitter, Metallic,Swirl, Pastel, Brush Tip, Fine Point

Methods Overview: Once you have selected your tool, you can try a number of techniques. However, depending on your method, you may need to rethink your medium. This is because different tools will help you accomplish specific coloring effects. Here are a few techniques for you to try.

Coloring: Tools of the Trade...Crayons and Beyond

Shading is accomplished with pressure. Color intensity is based on light pressure placed on the paper using your chosen medium. Generally, this technique should be light enough to allow the paper (white) to show through the color.

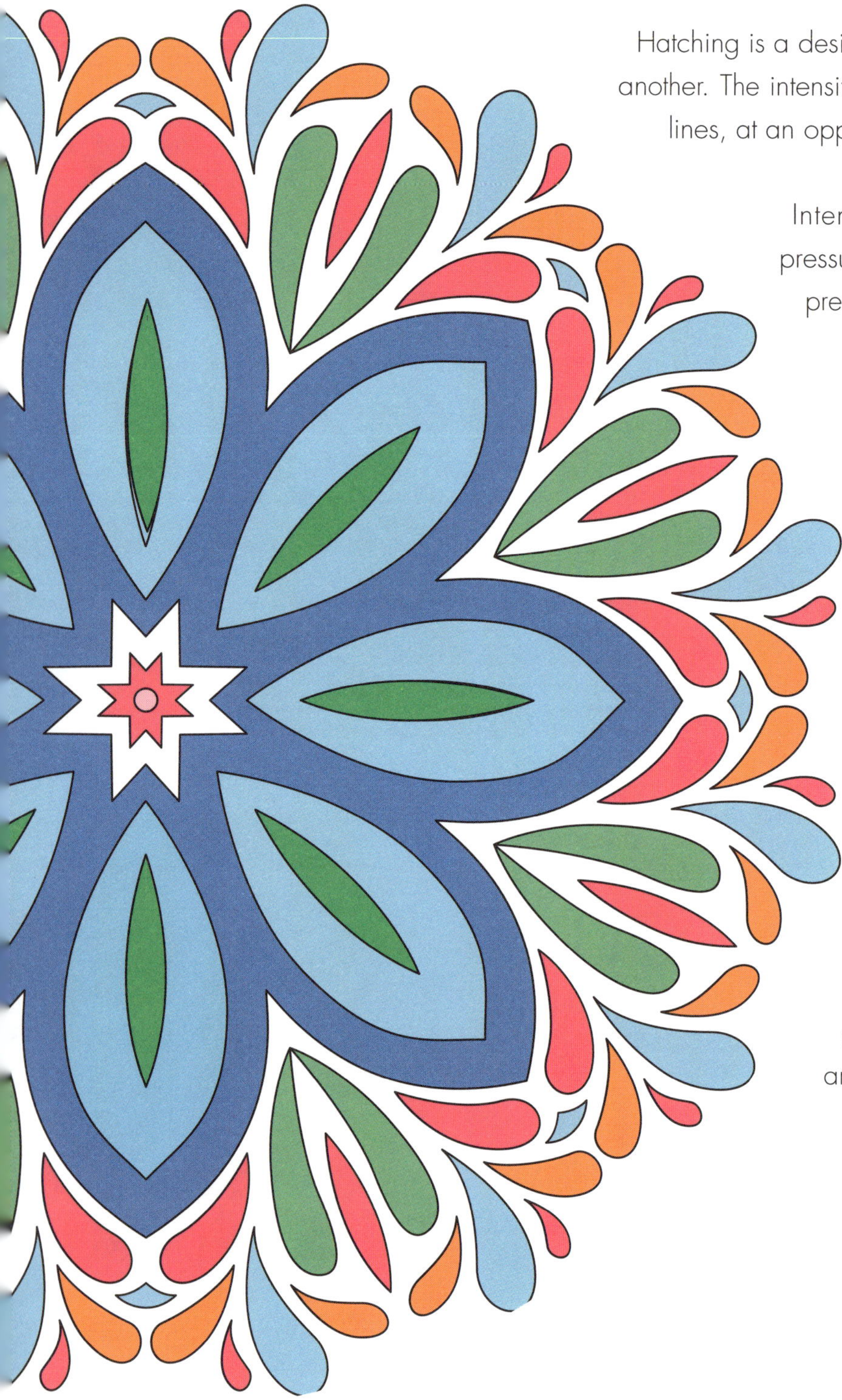

Hatching is a design element created by lines drawn parallel to one another. The intensity of the color can be added by drawing parallel lines, at an opposing angle, on top of the first lines drawn.

Intensity of color is determined by the degree of pressure placed on the page using your color tool. This pressure creates the level of bright or bold color.

Coloring Tips:

Mind Your Mood: Science has revealed that color tells on us. Be mindful of your selection when determining your goal for the project.

Slow or Speedy: Don't color fast. This is not a race. If you build color slowly, you can watch the color evolve and create the intensity of color you want.

Reap the Reward: Let your excitement build as you get to see the final result. Consider going "beyond the fridge" and framing your artwork to enjoy long-term.

Color Swatches... Test Your Color

Color Swatches...Test Your Color

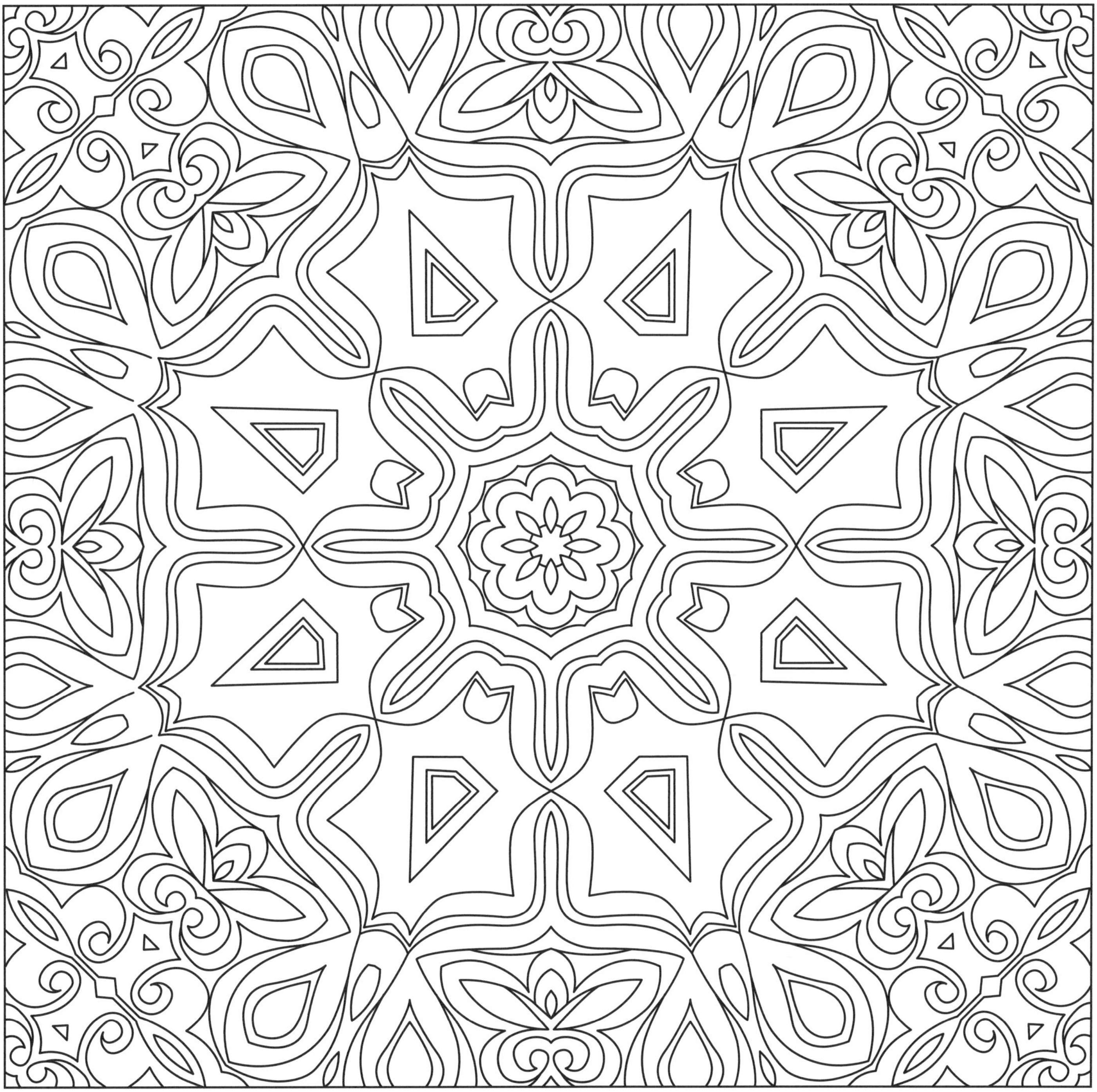

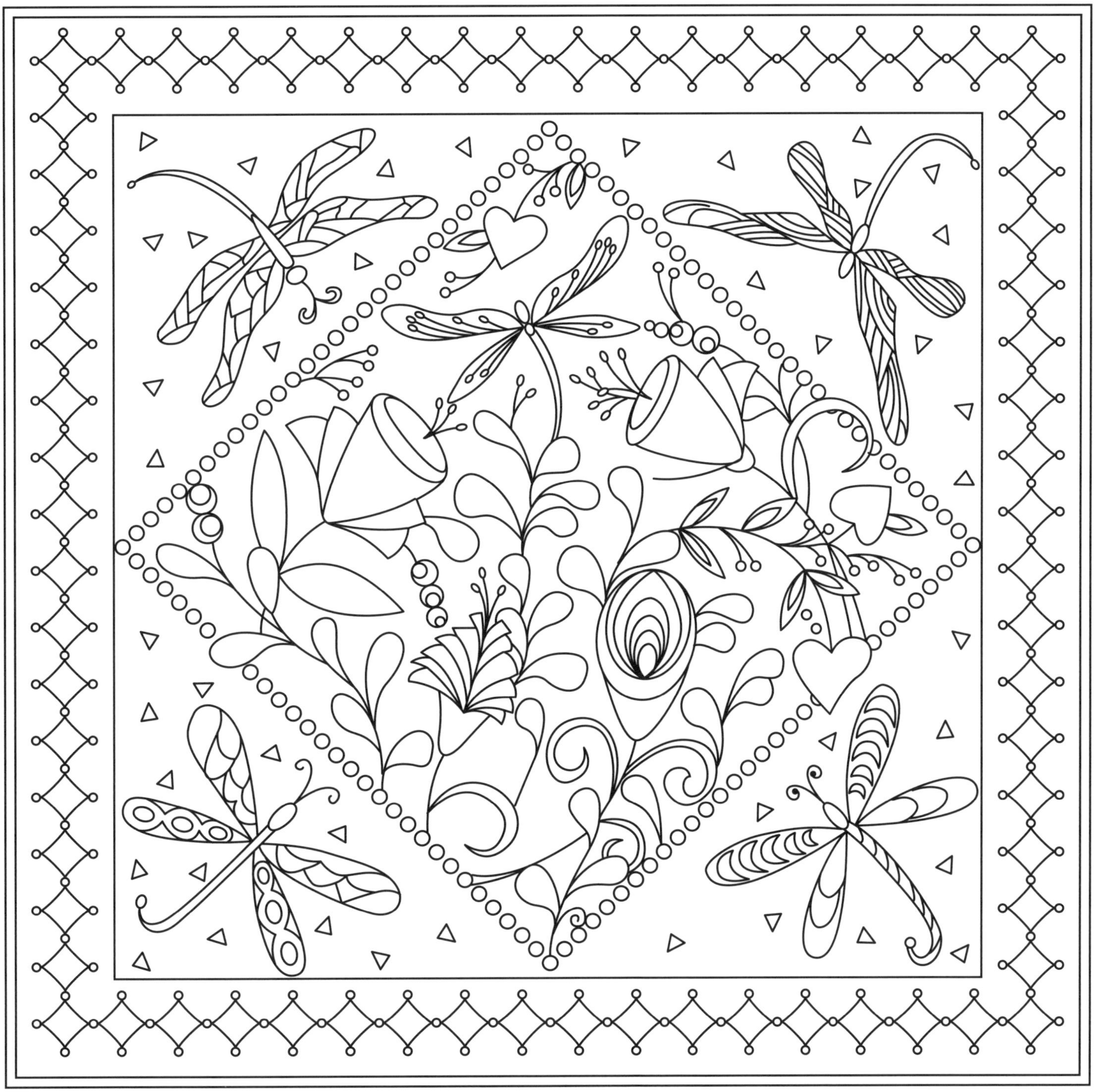

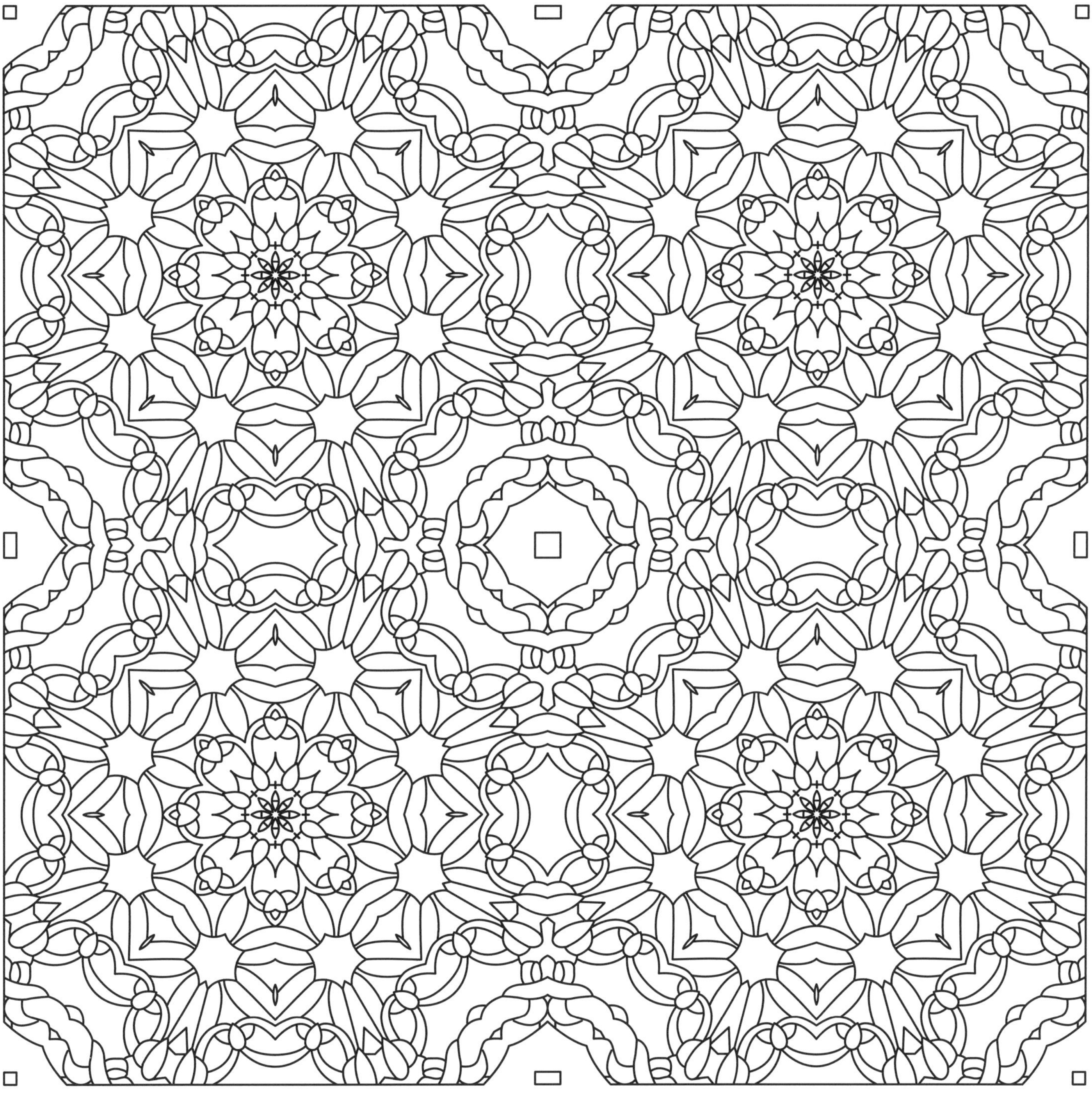

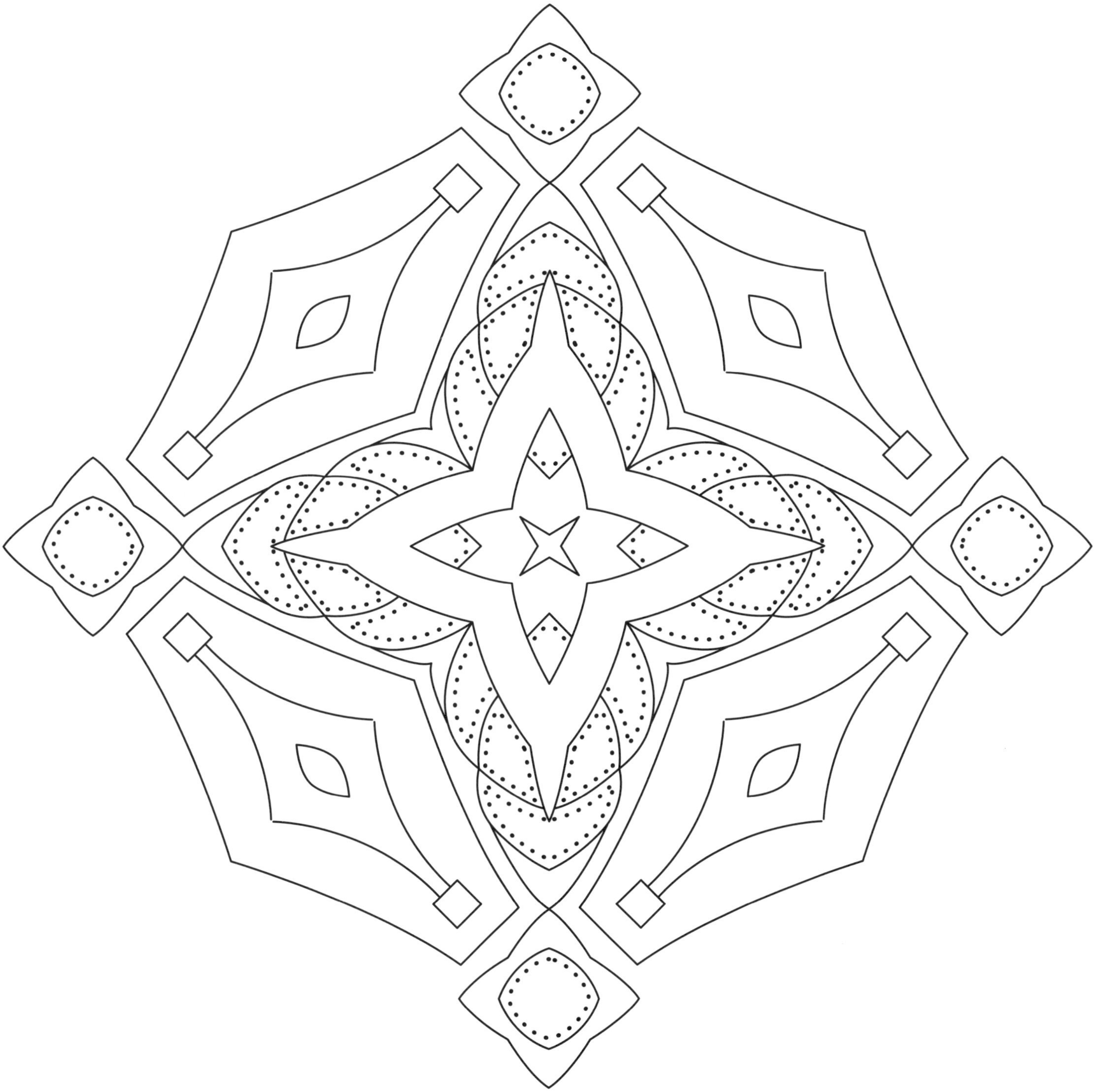

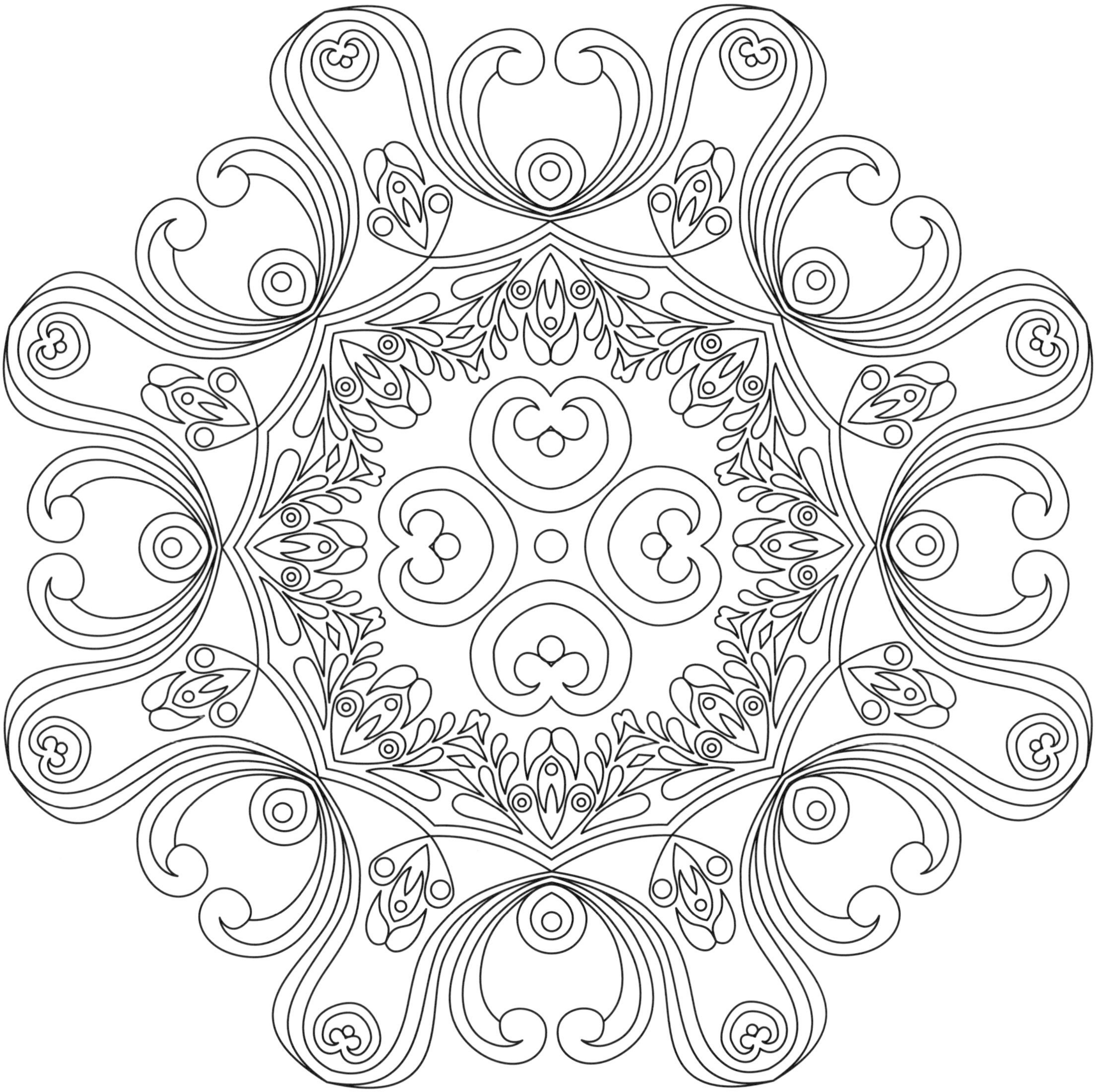

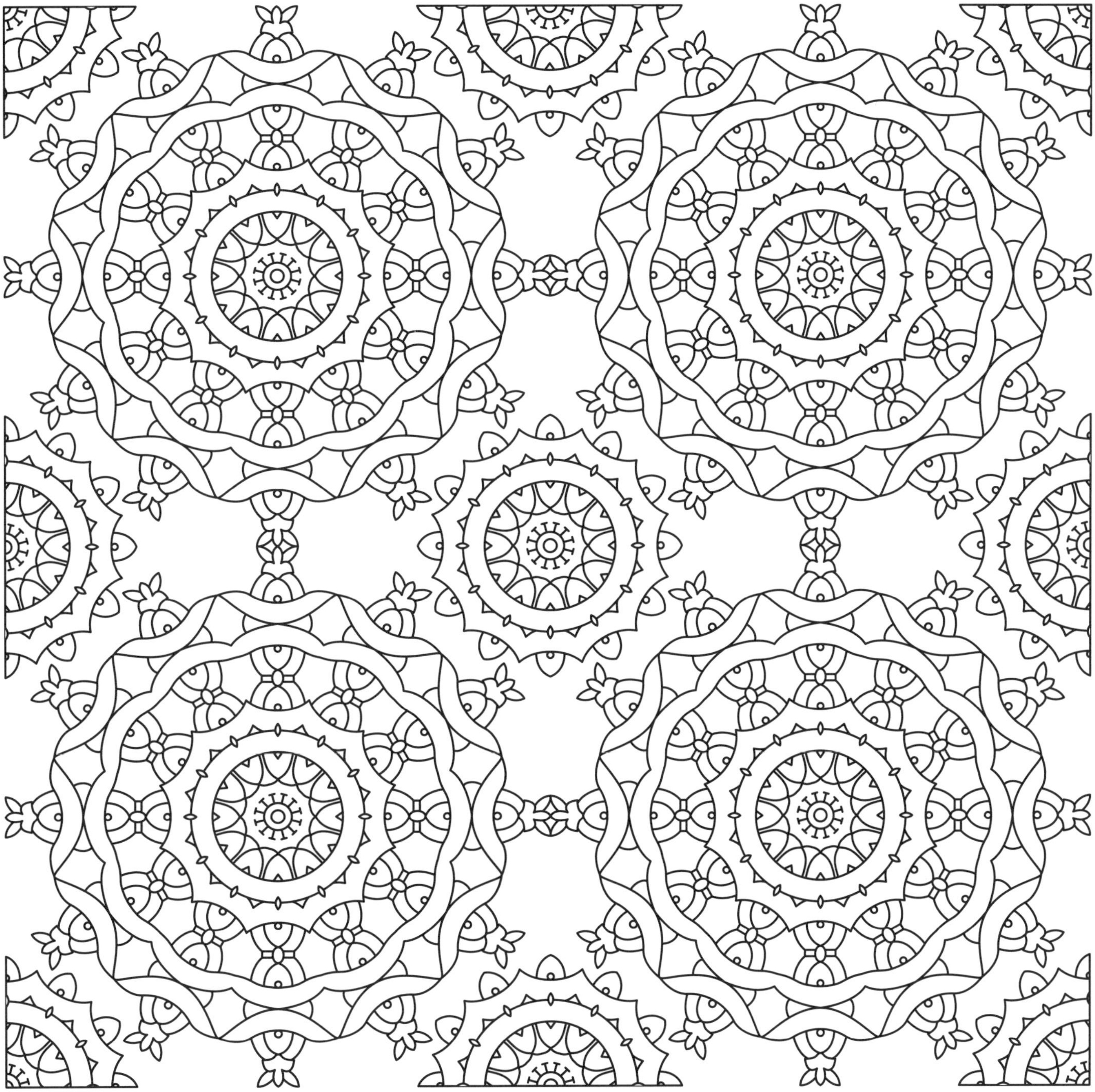

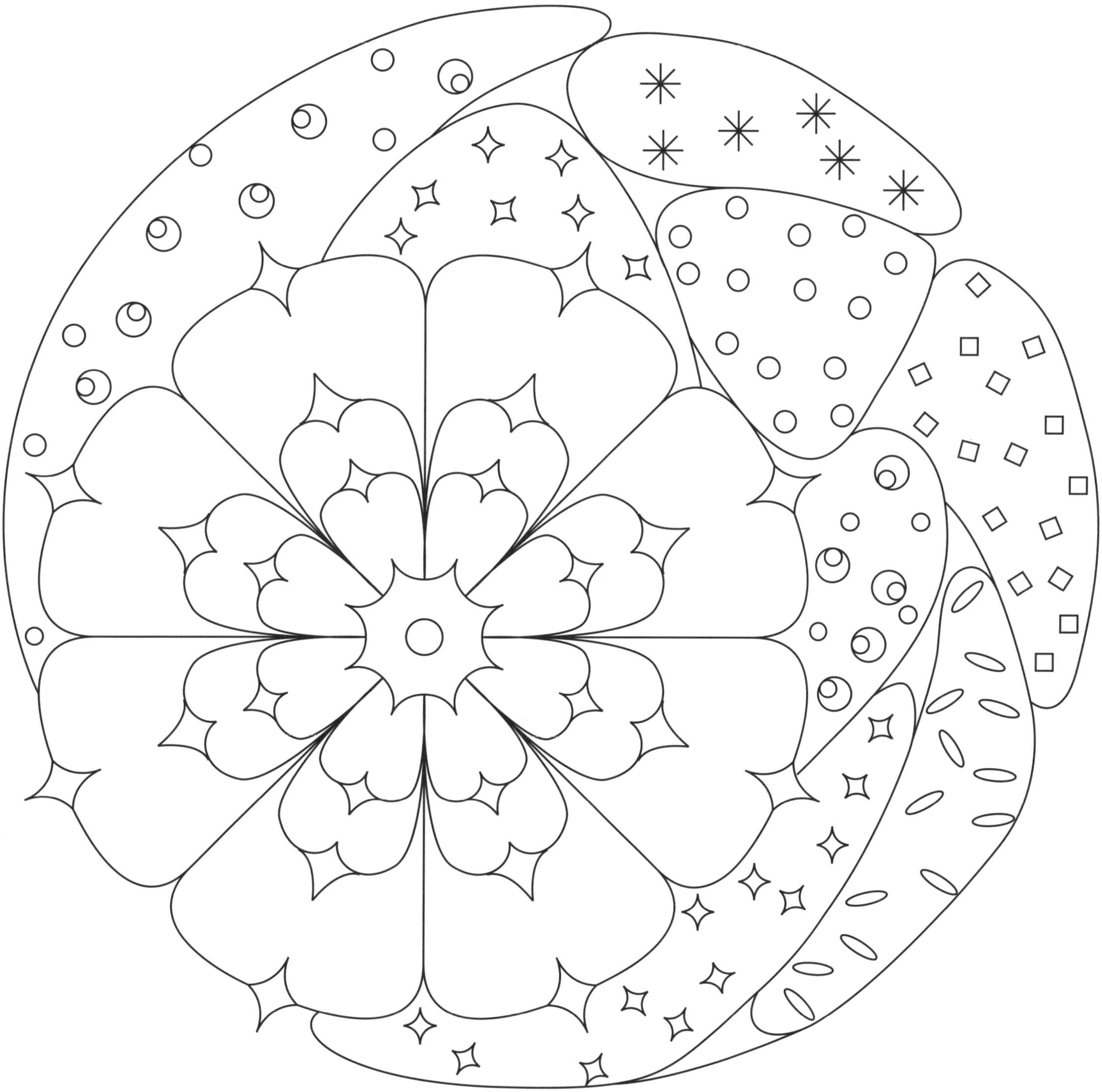

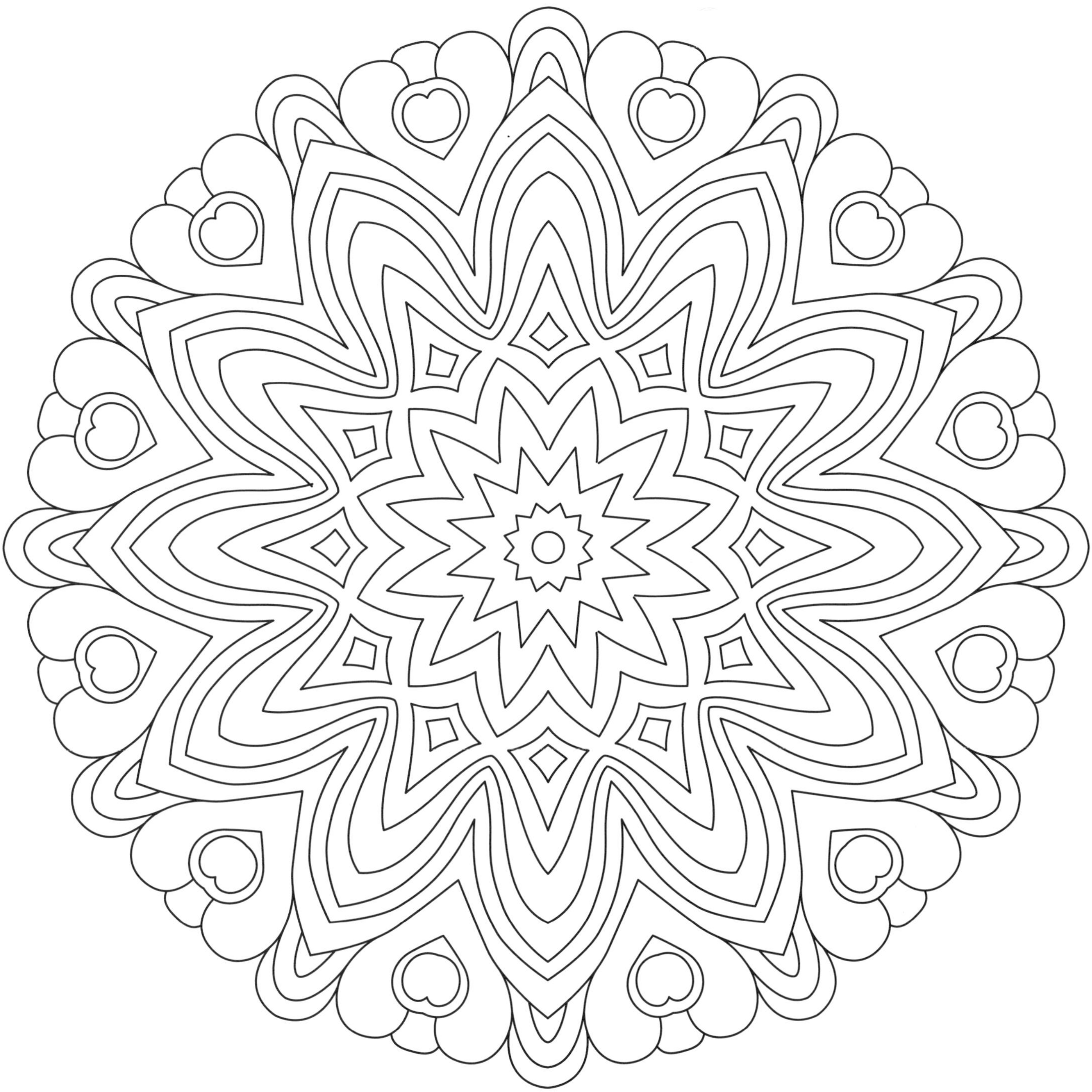

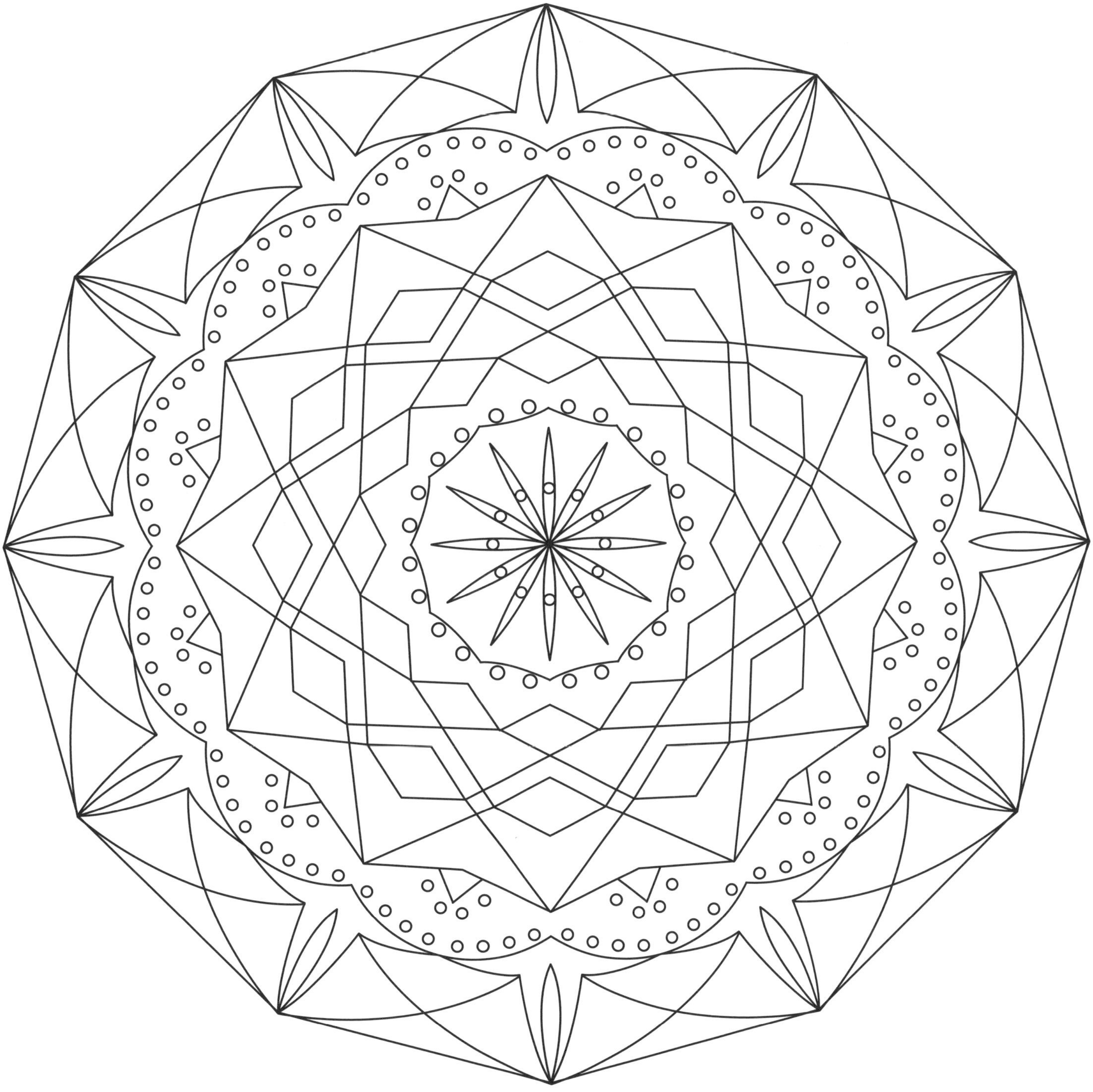

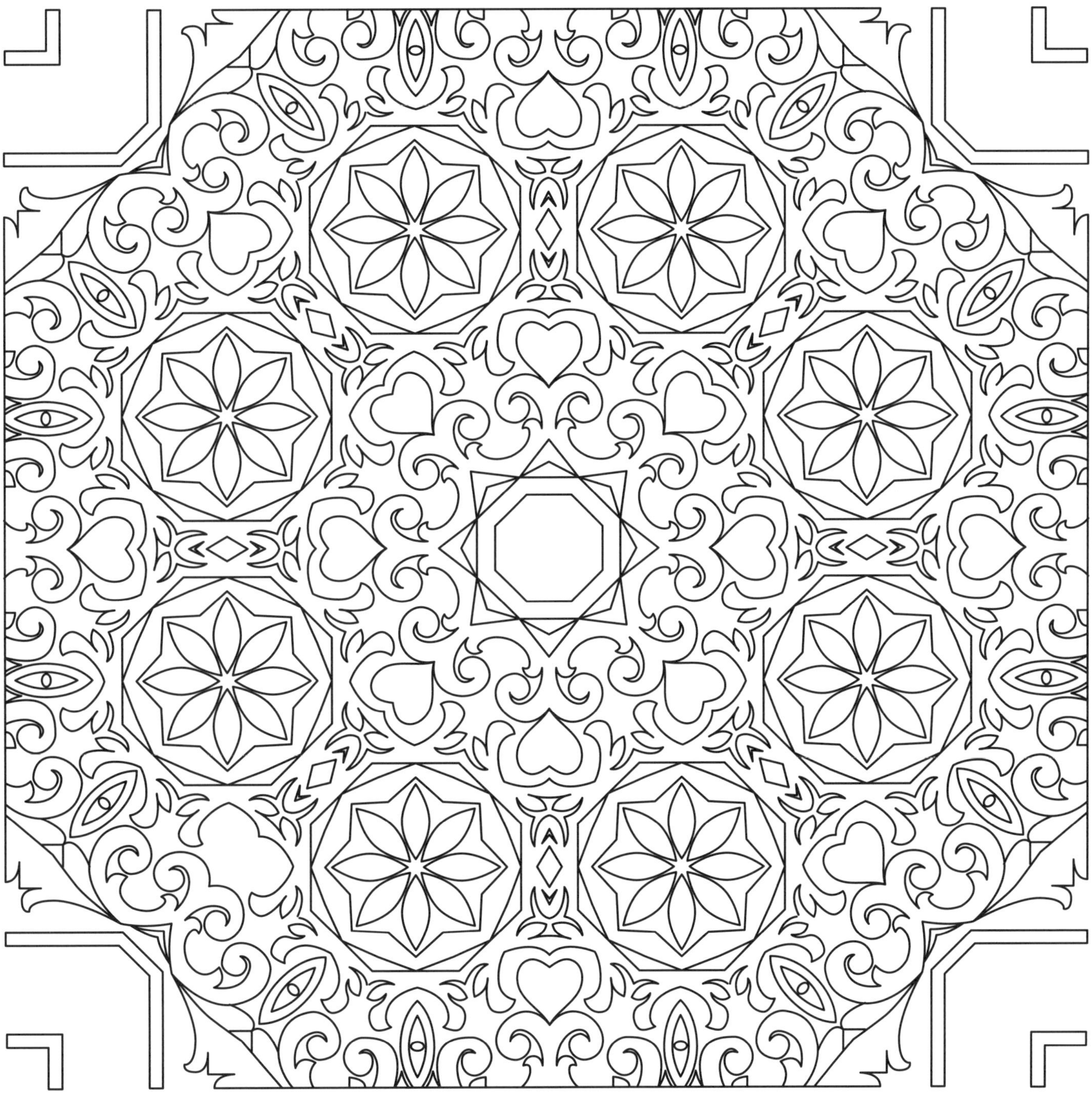

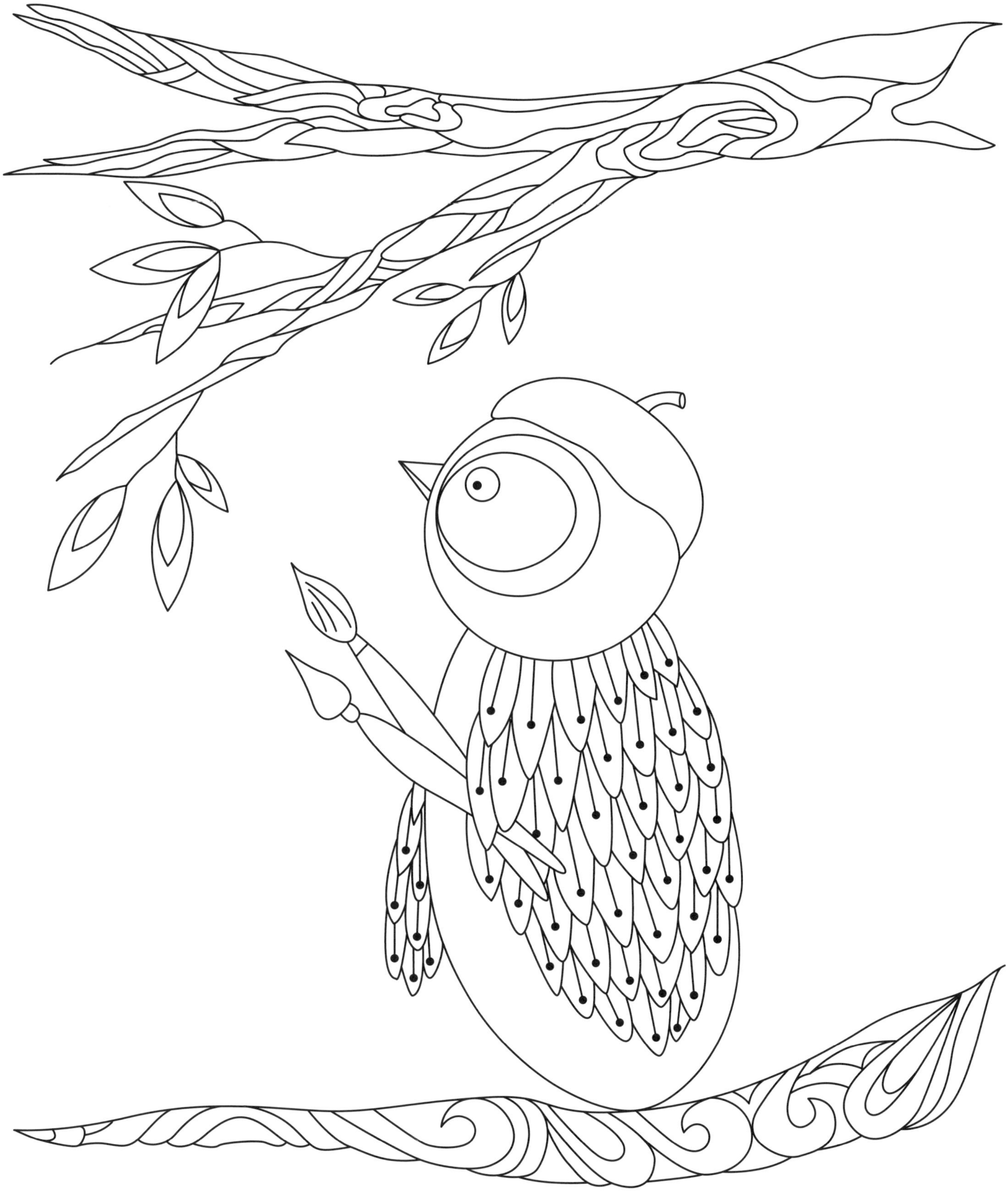

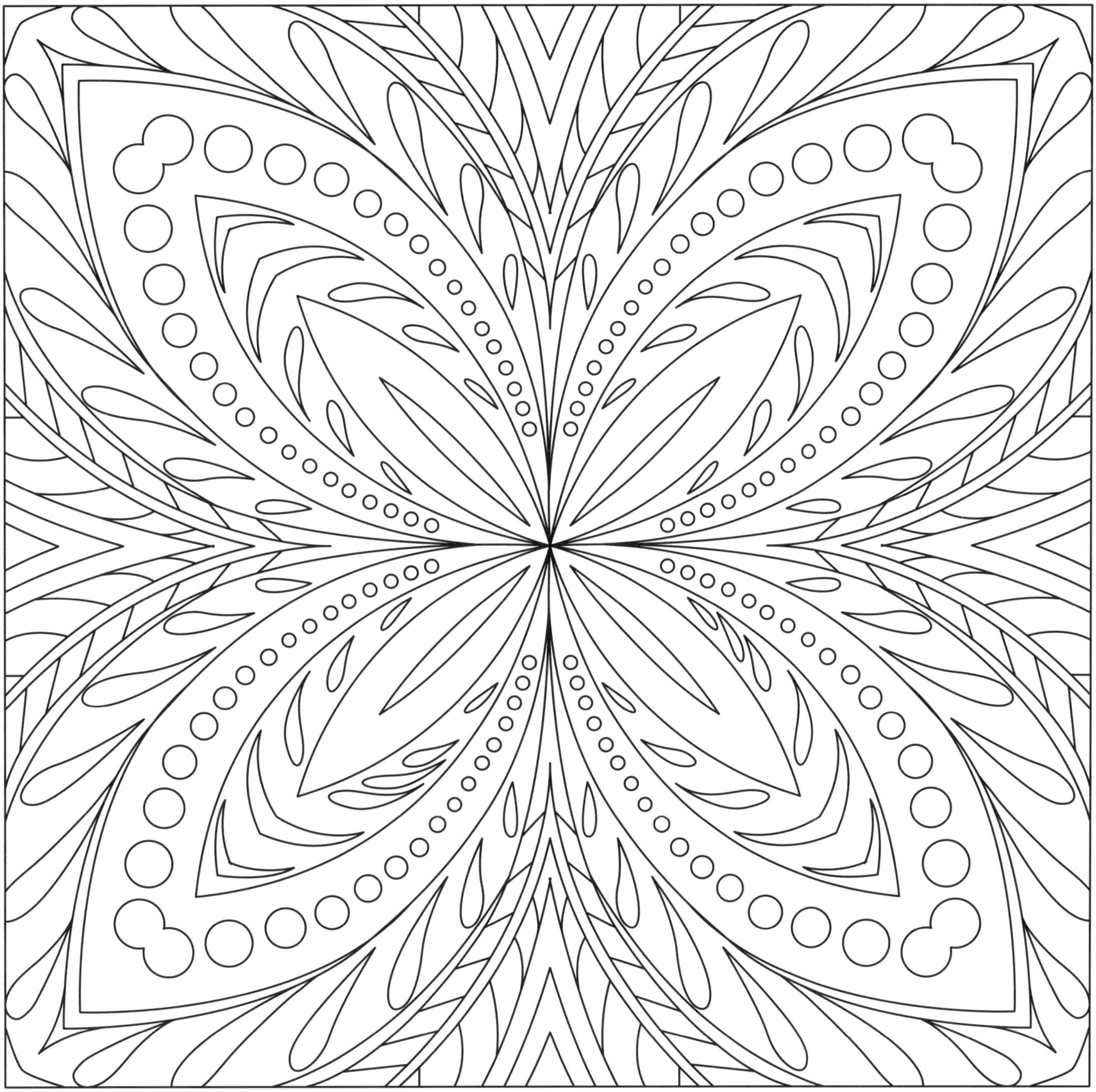

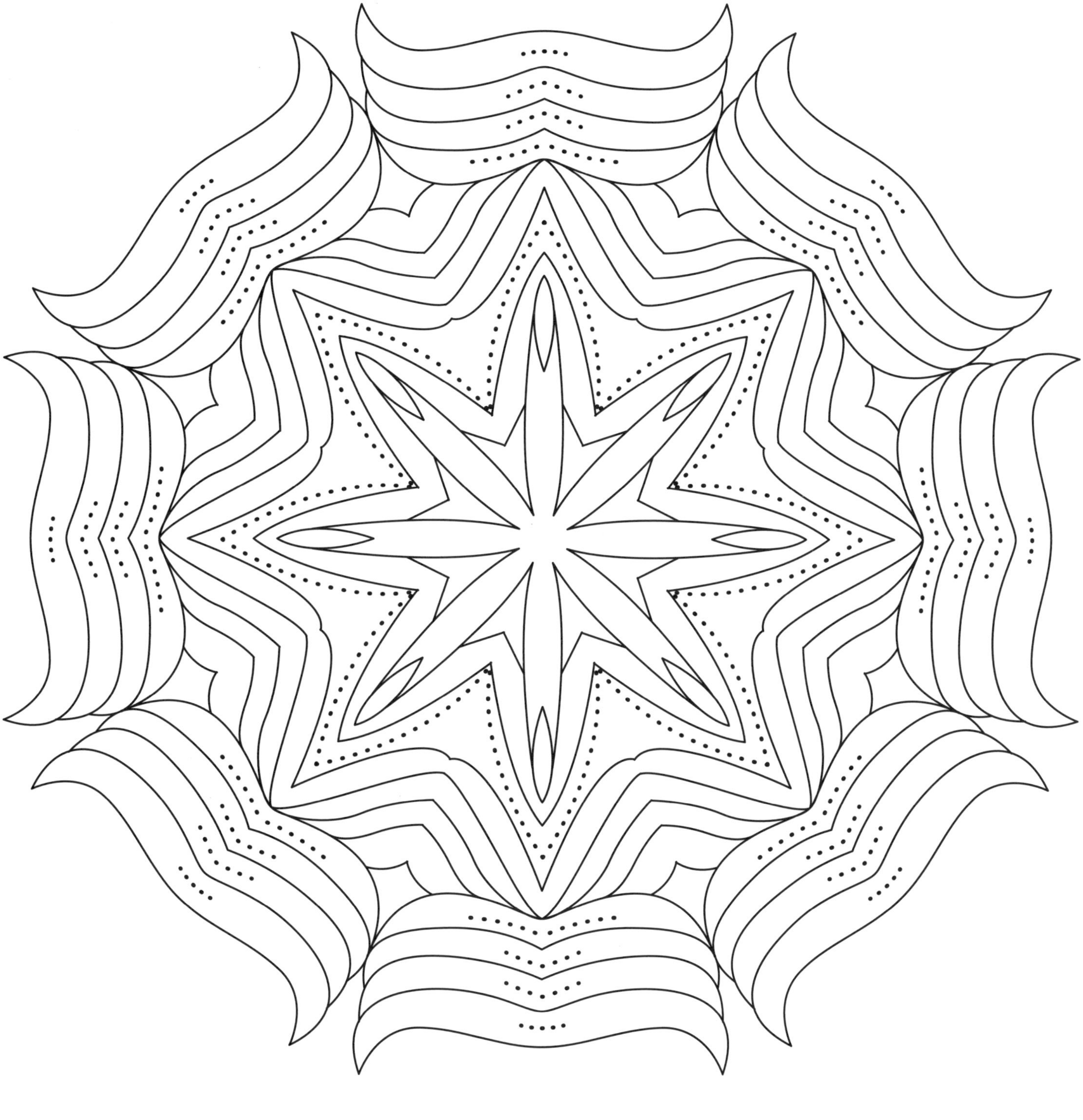

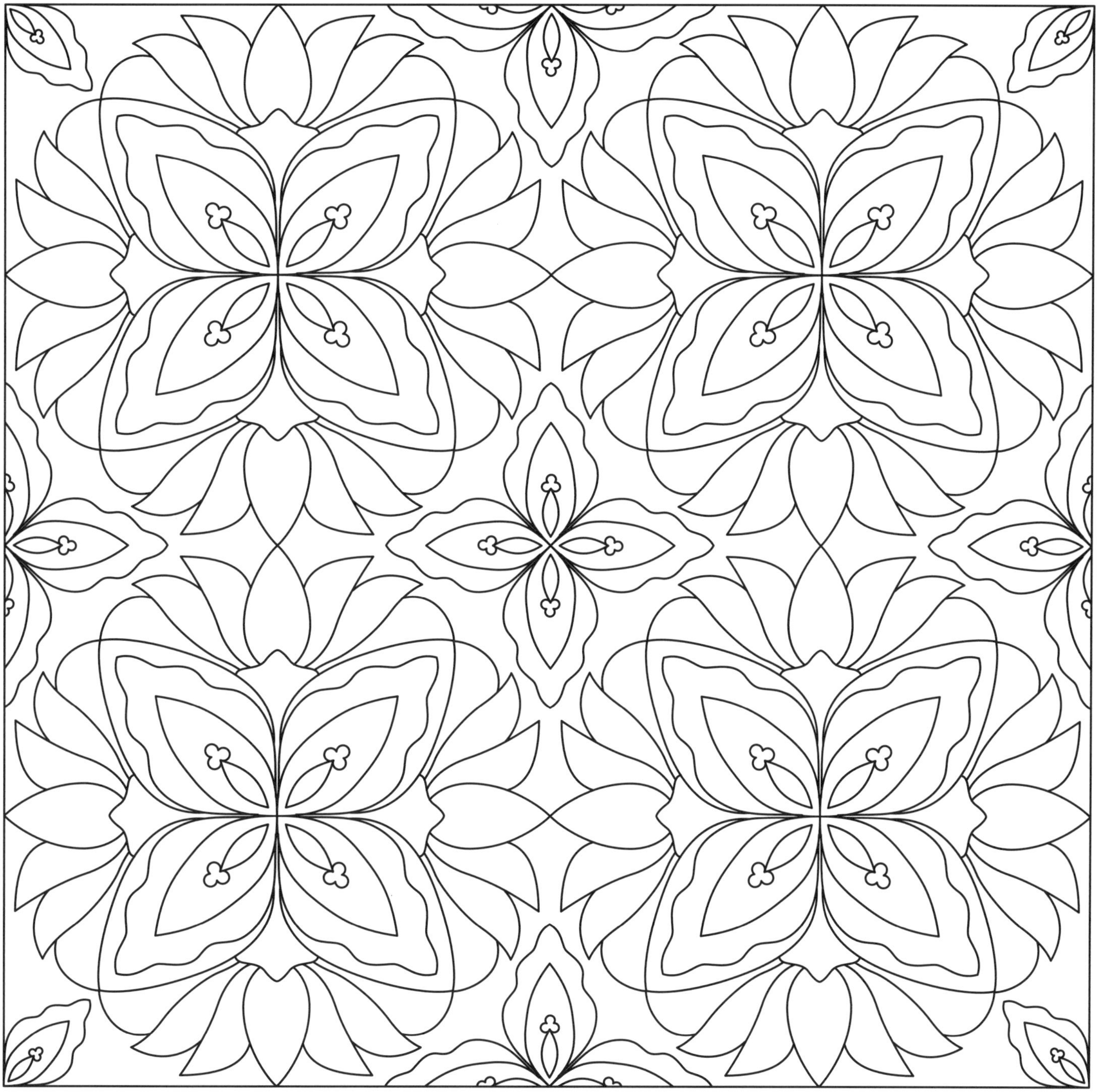

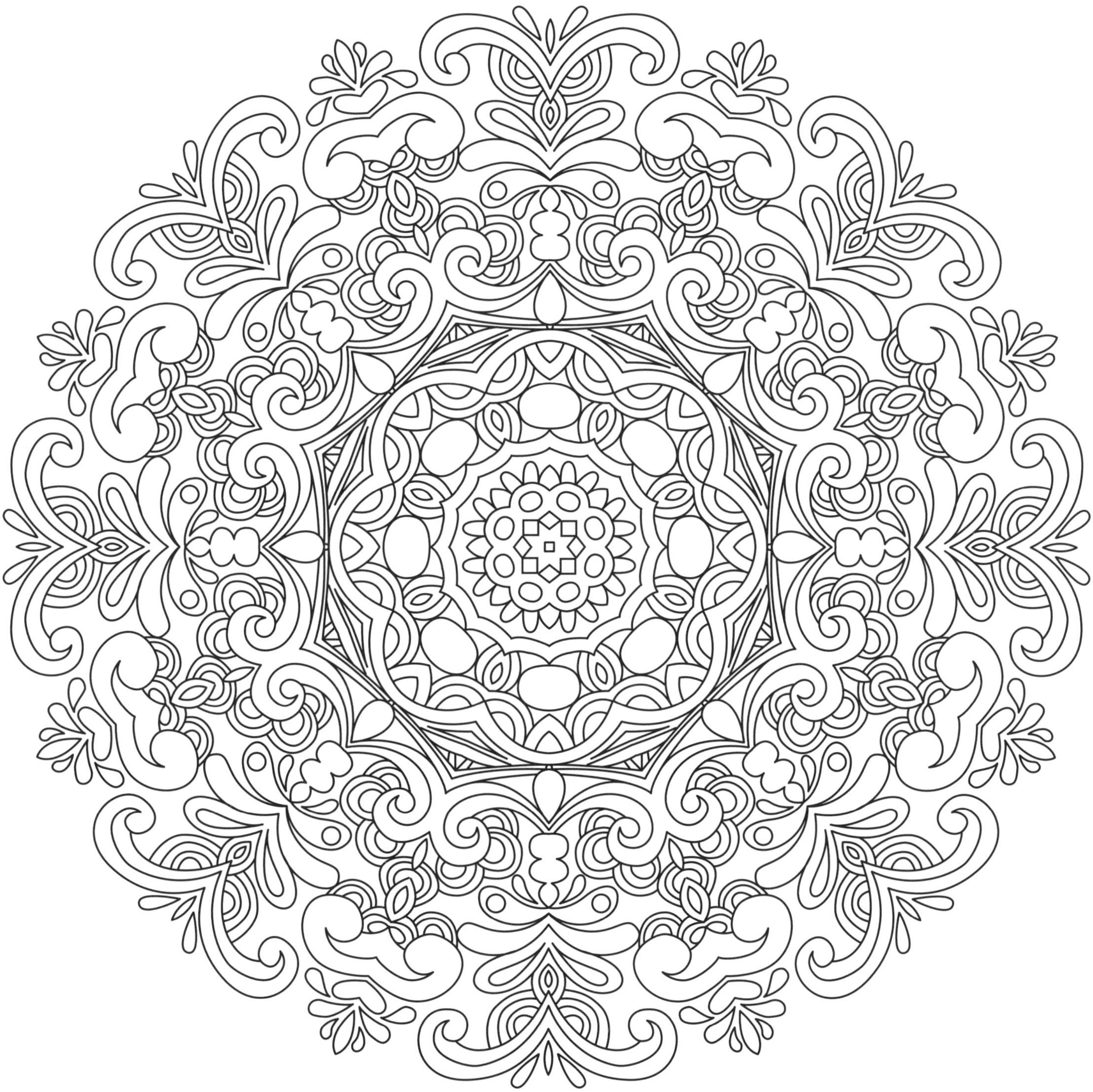

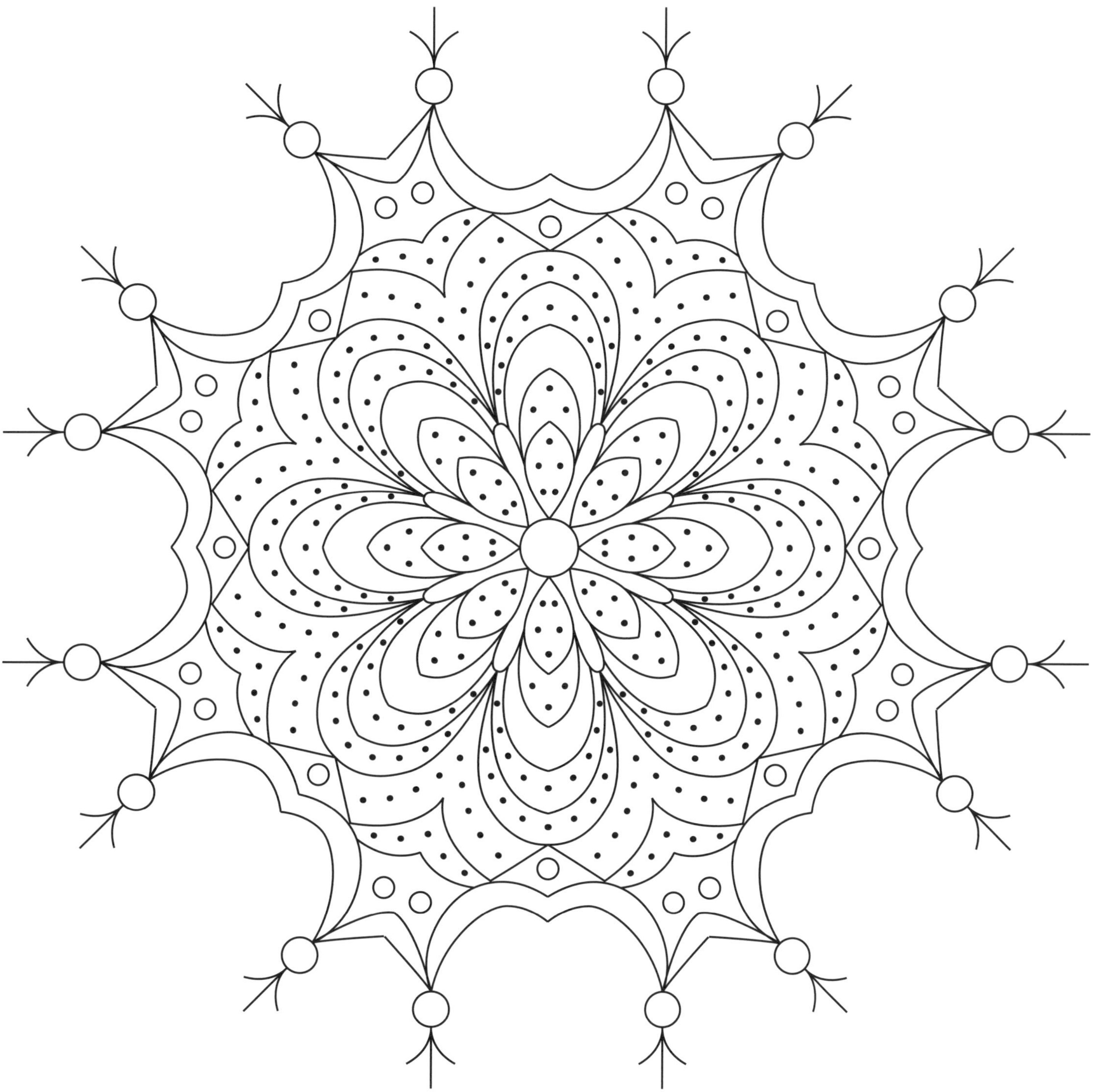

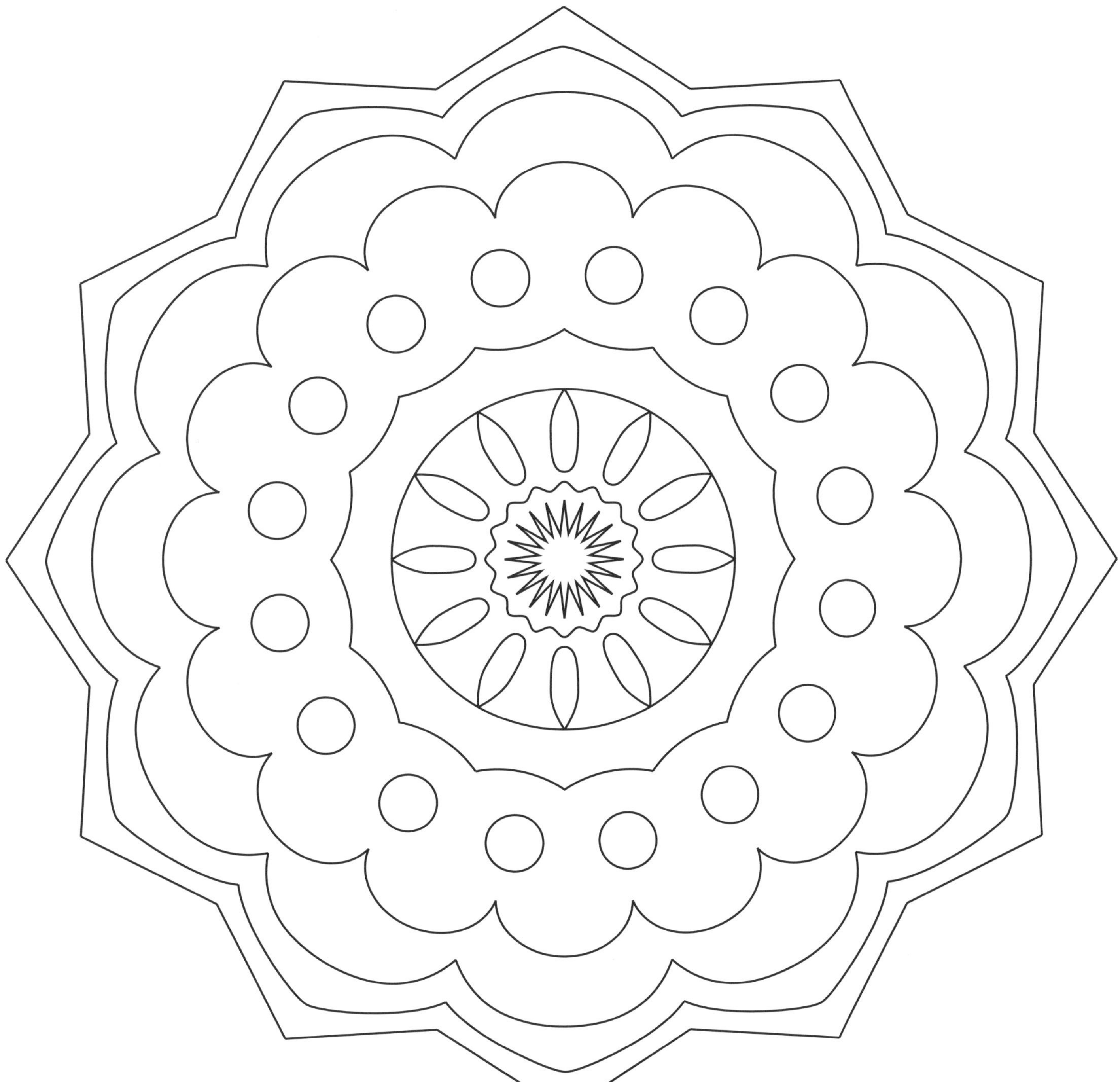

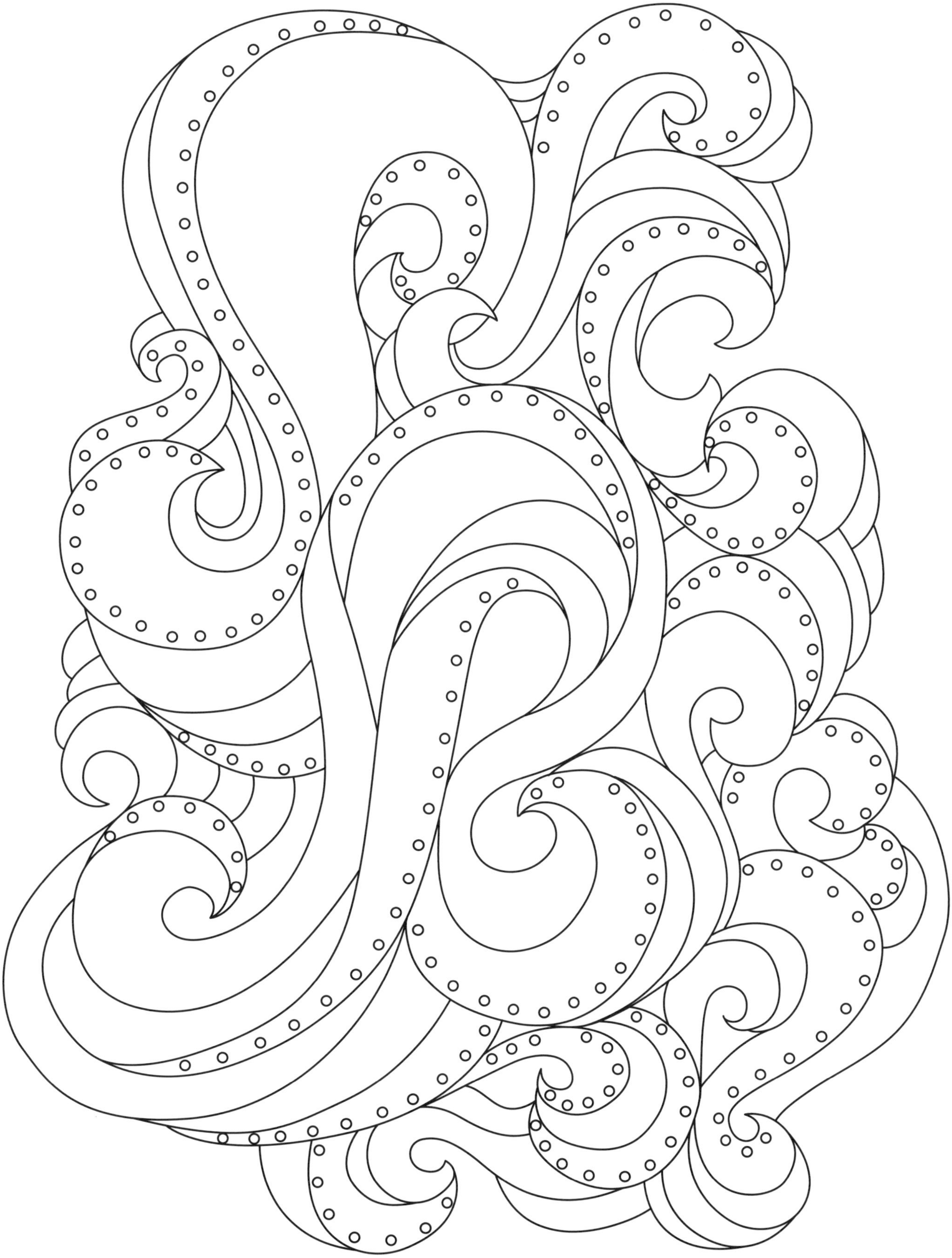

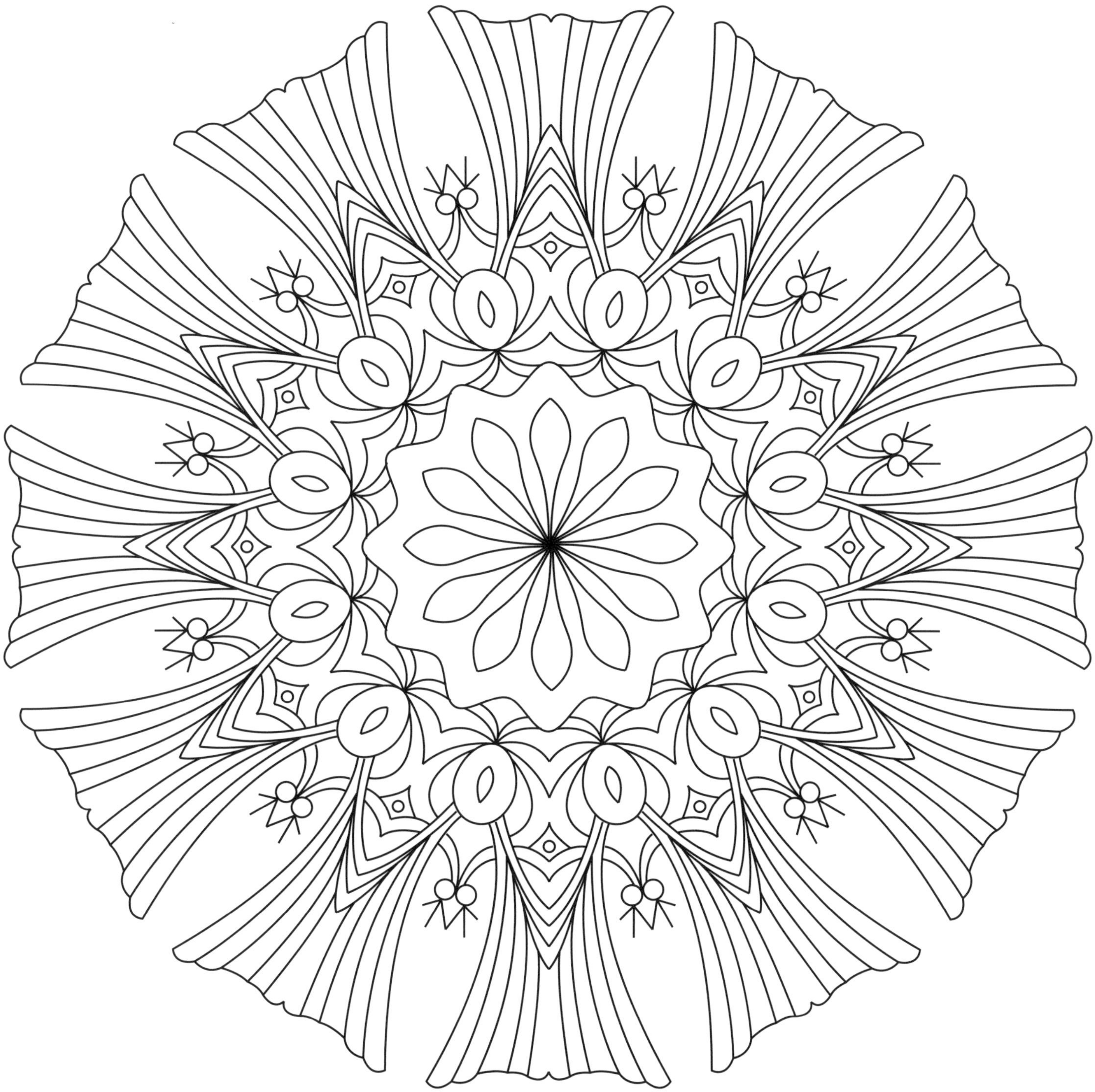

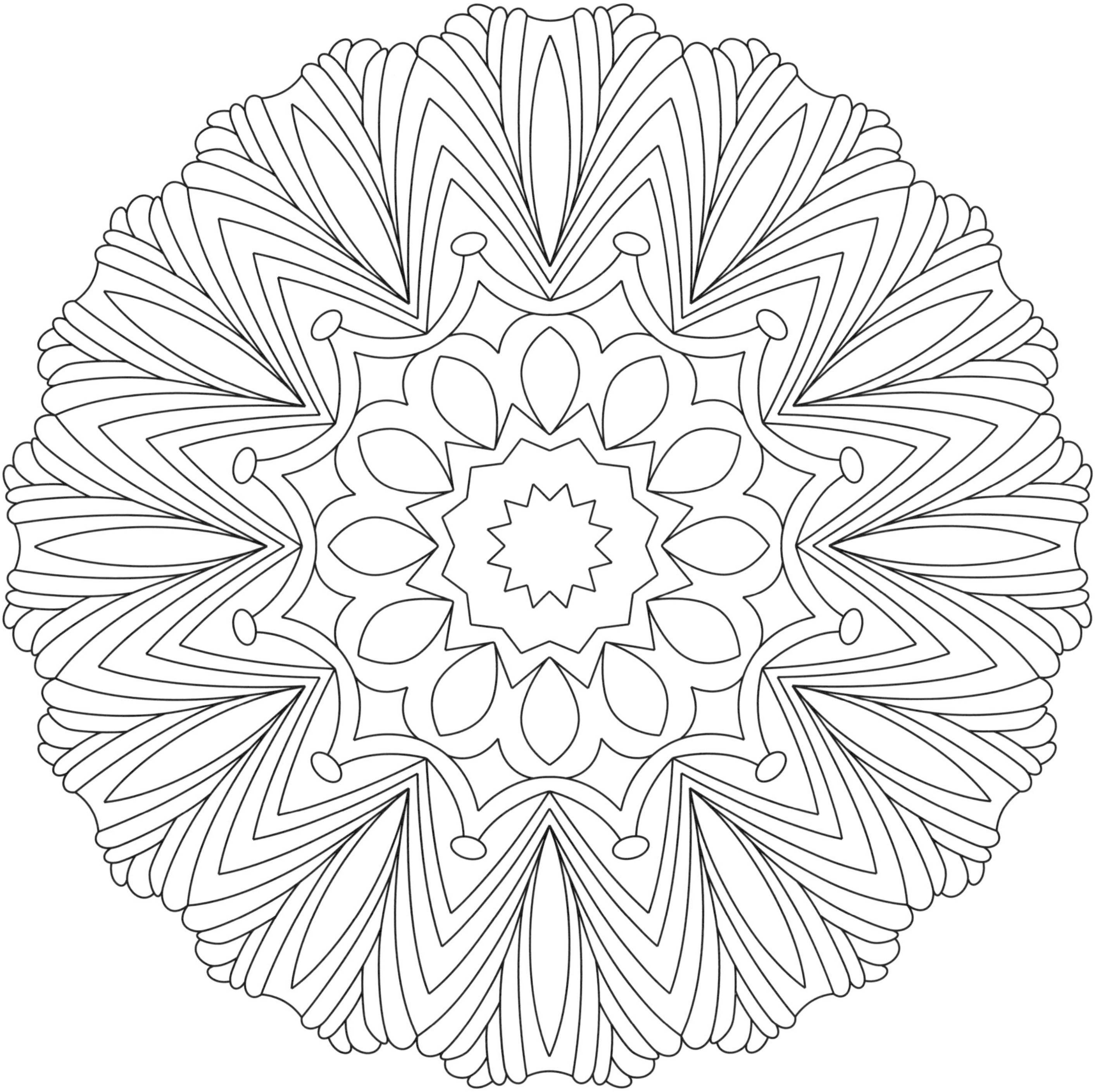

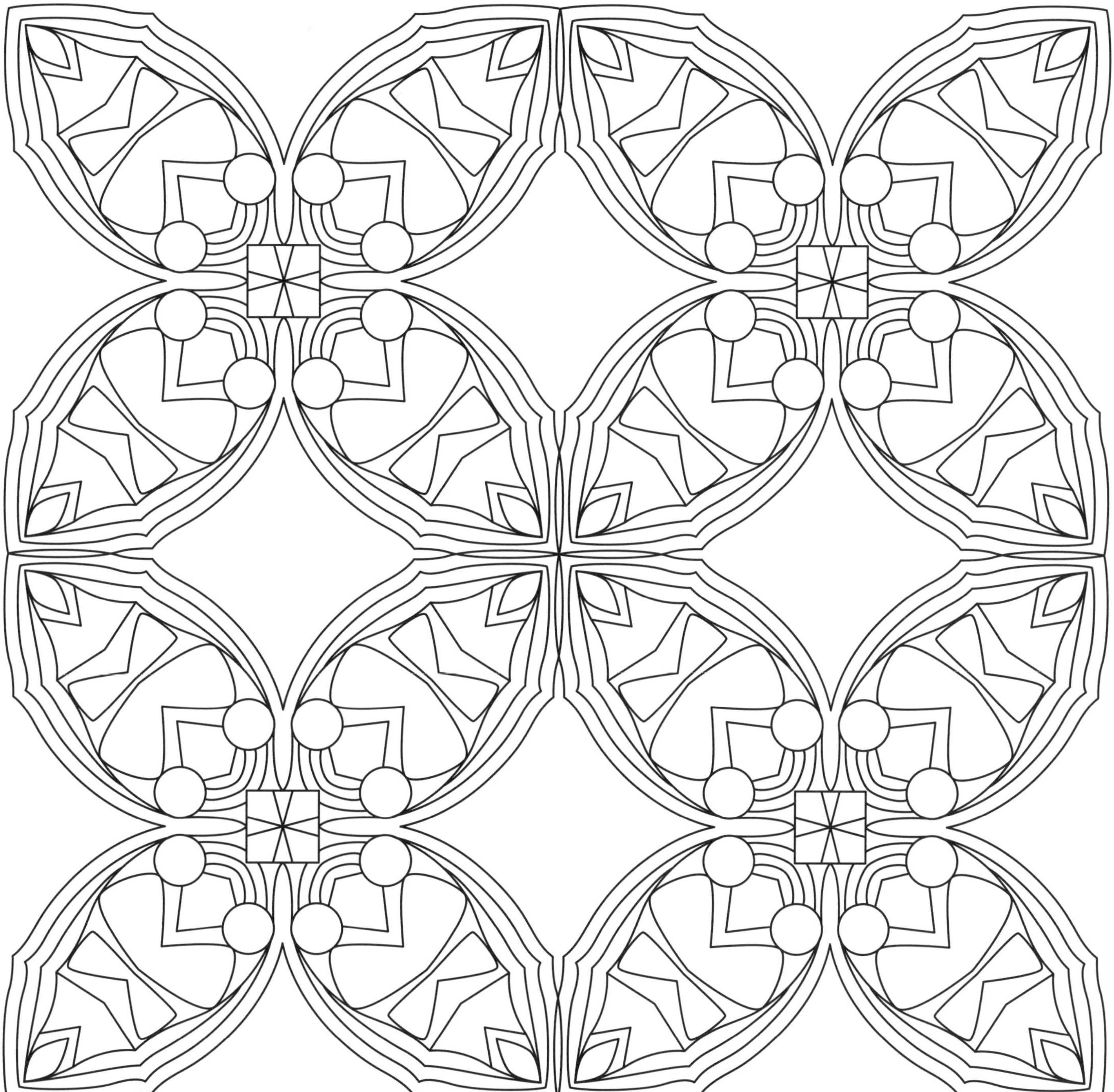

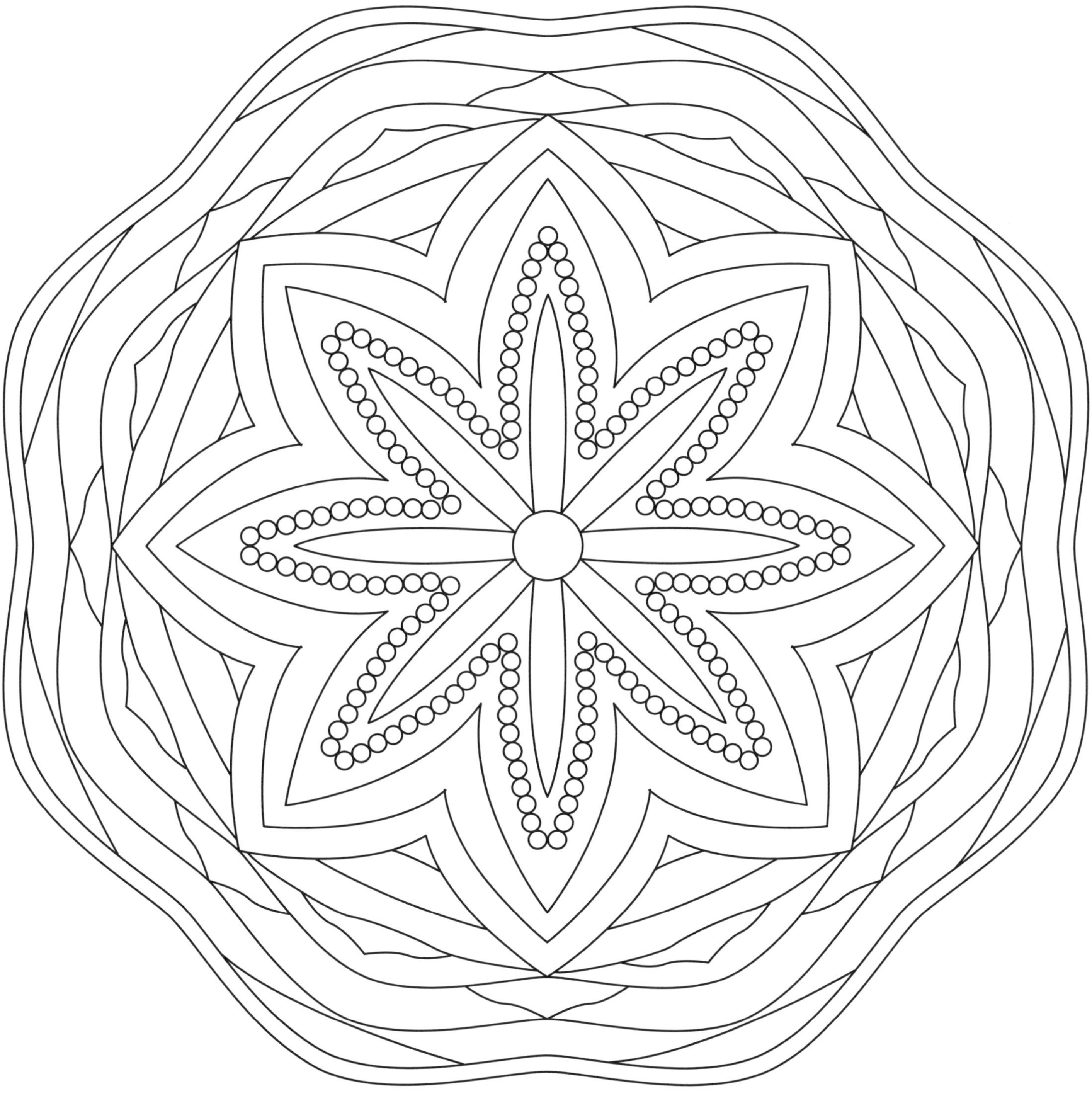

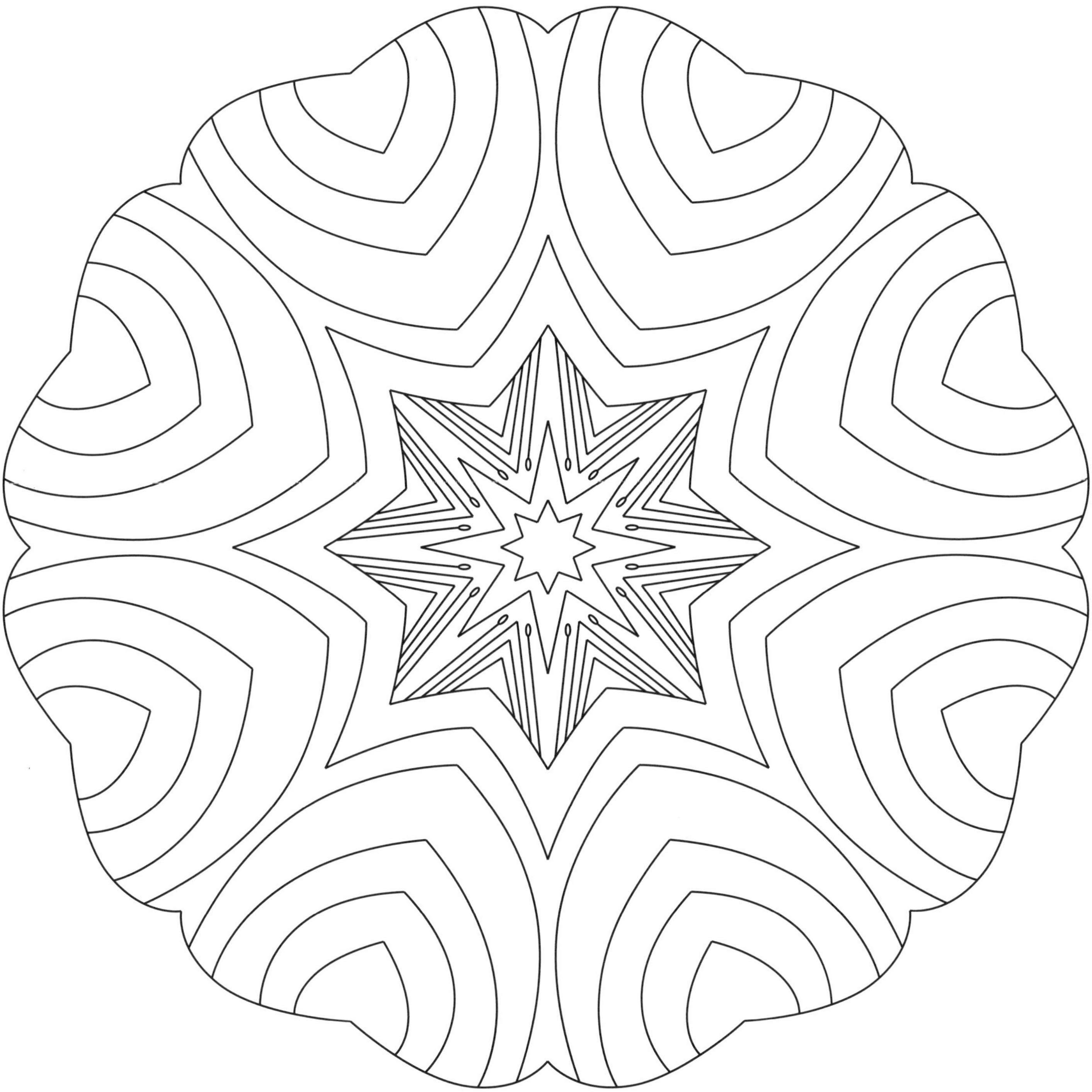

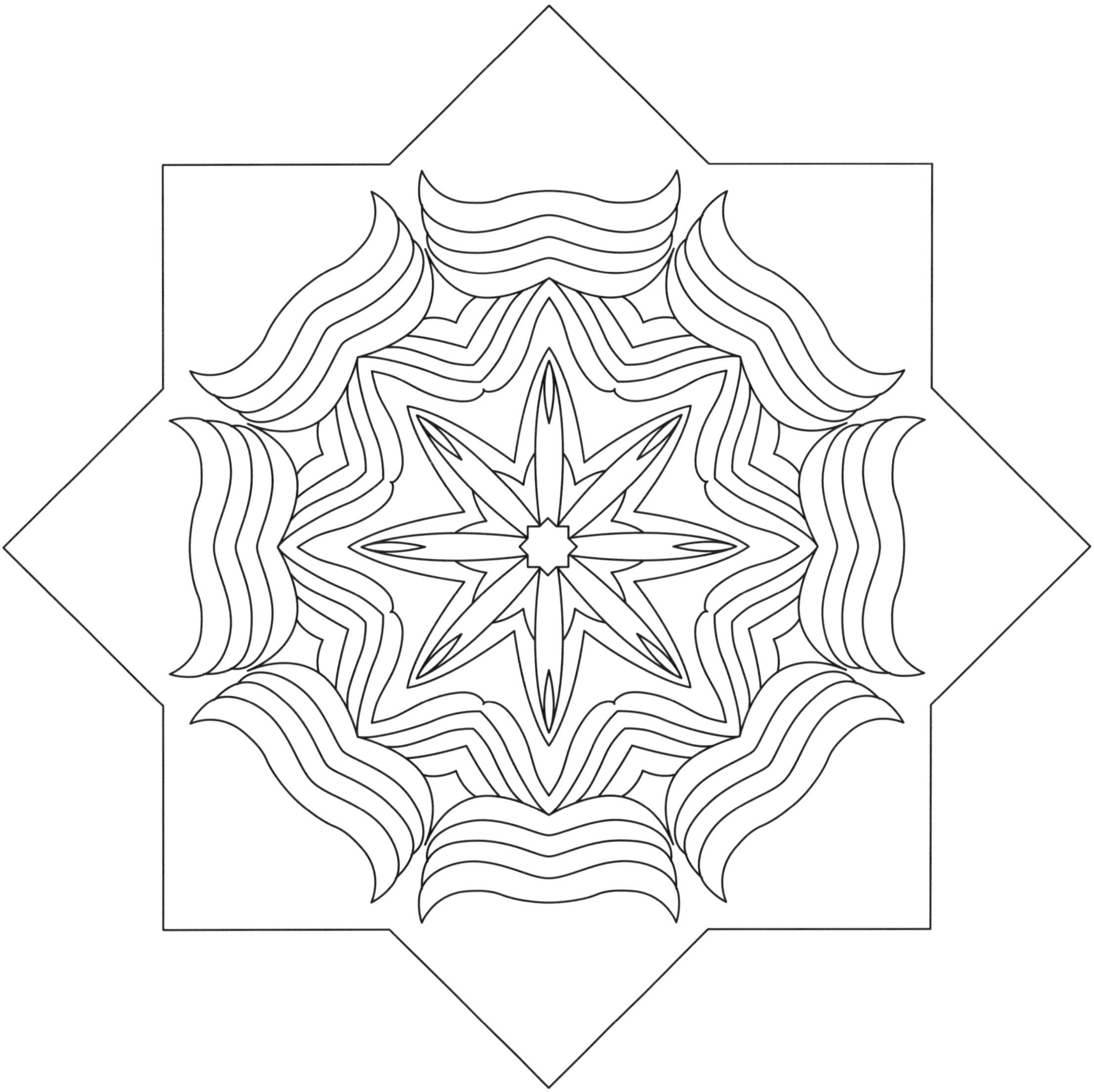

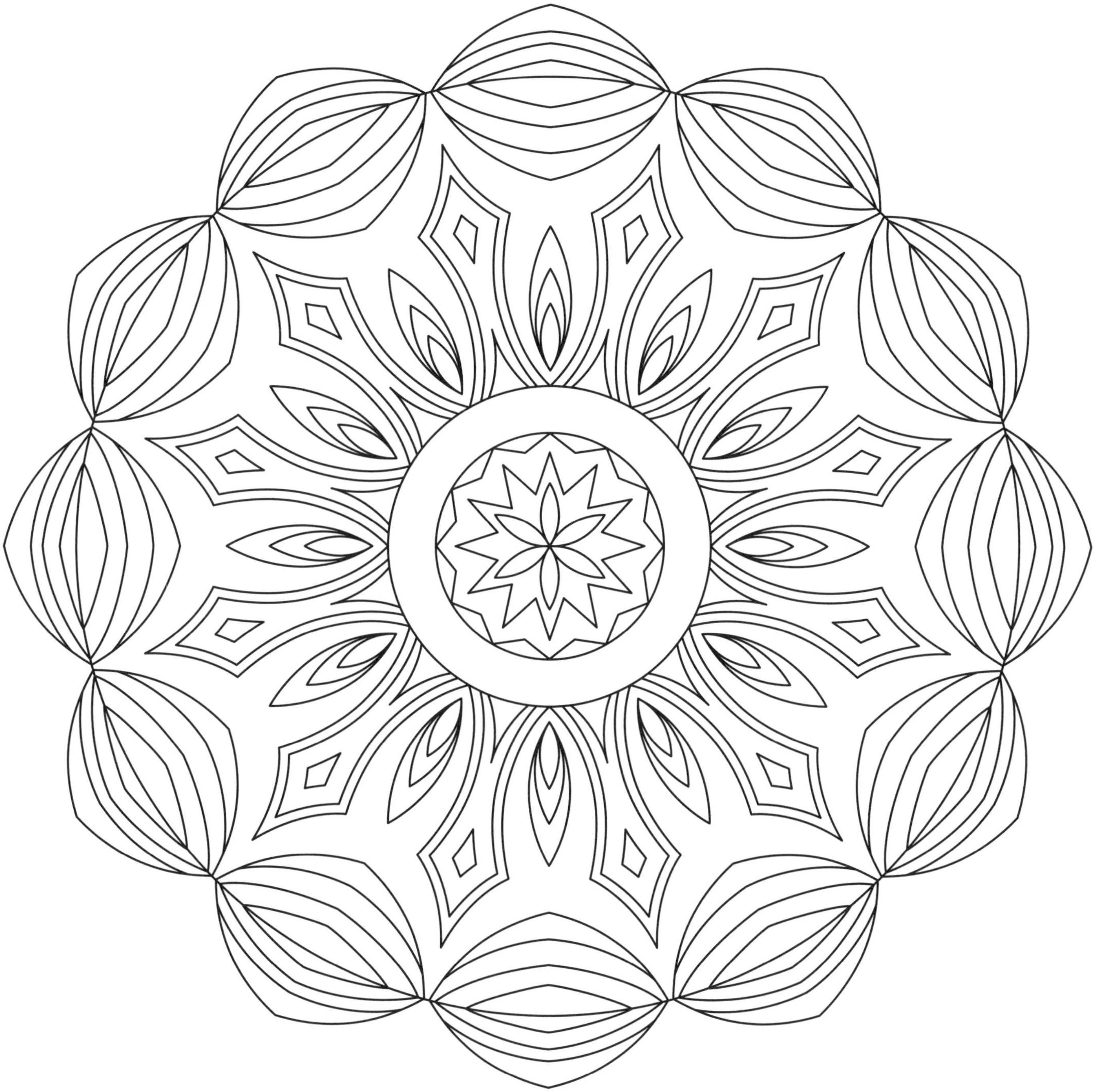

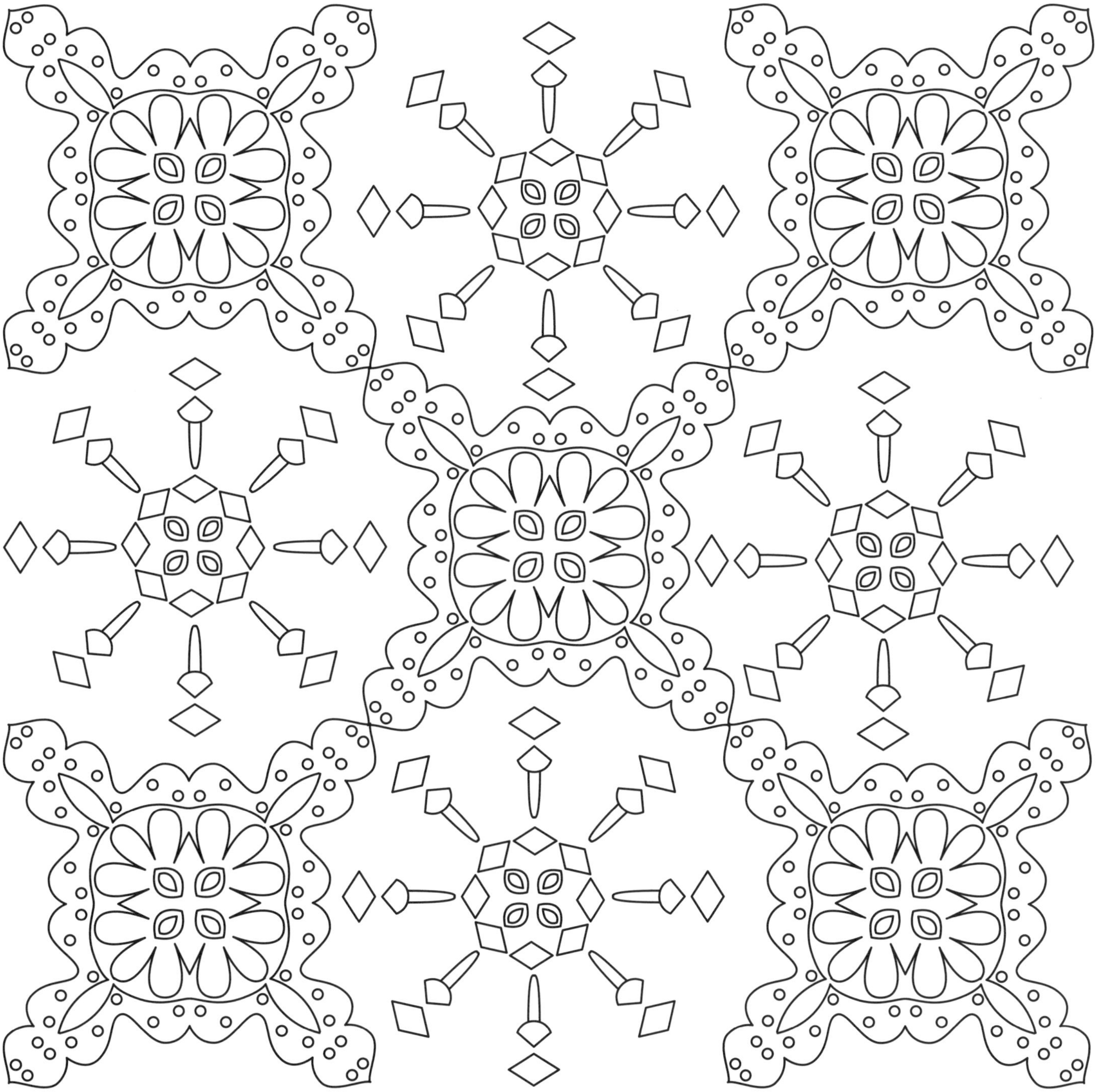

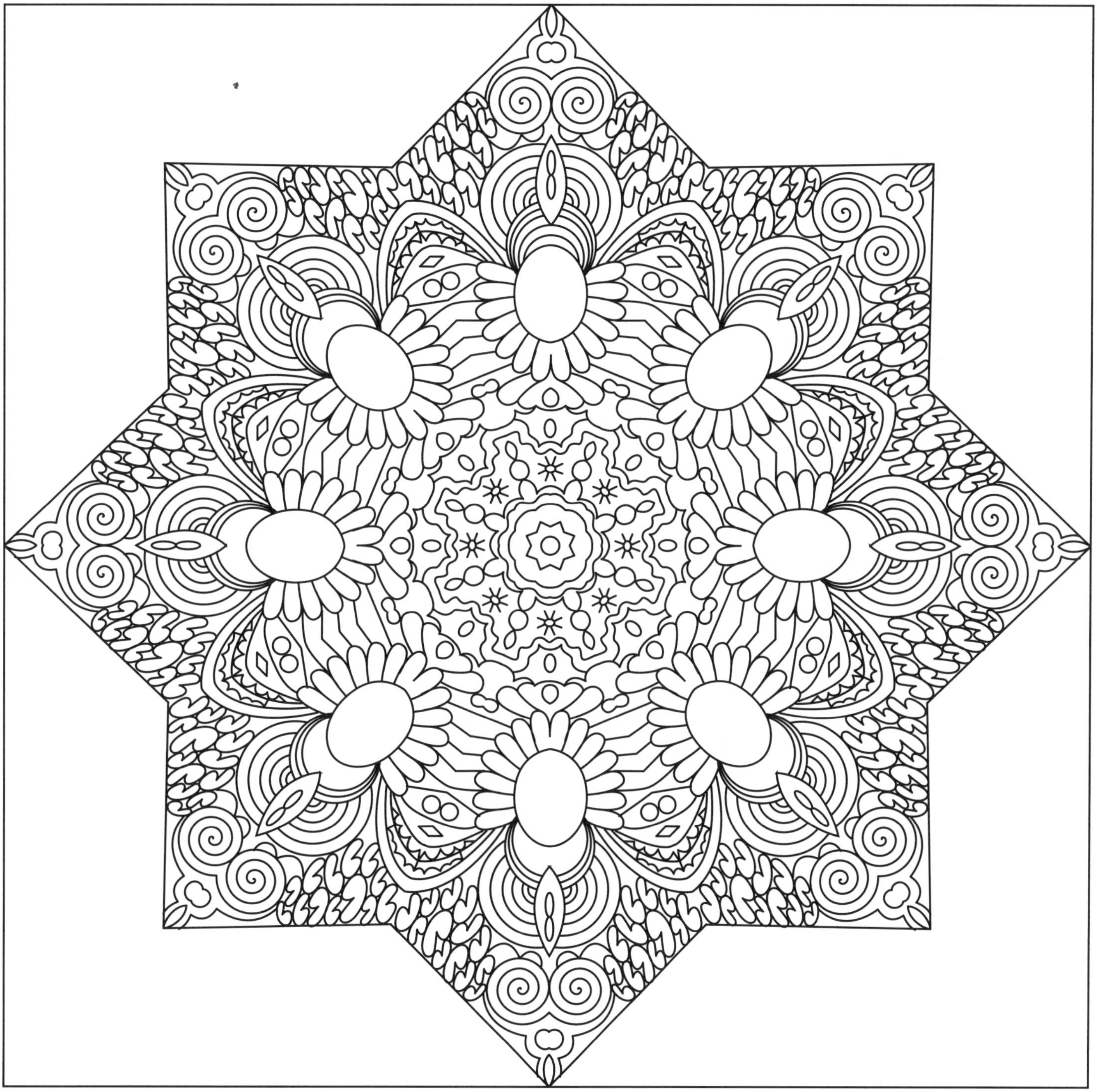

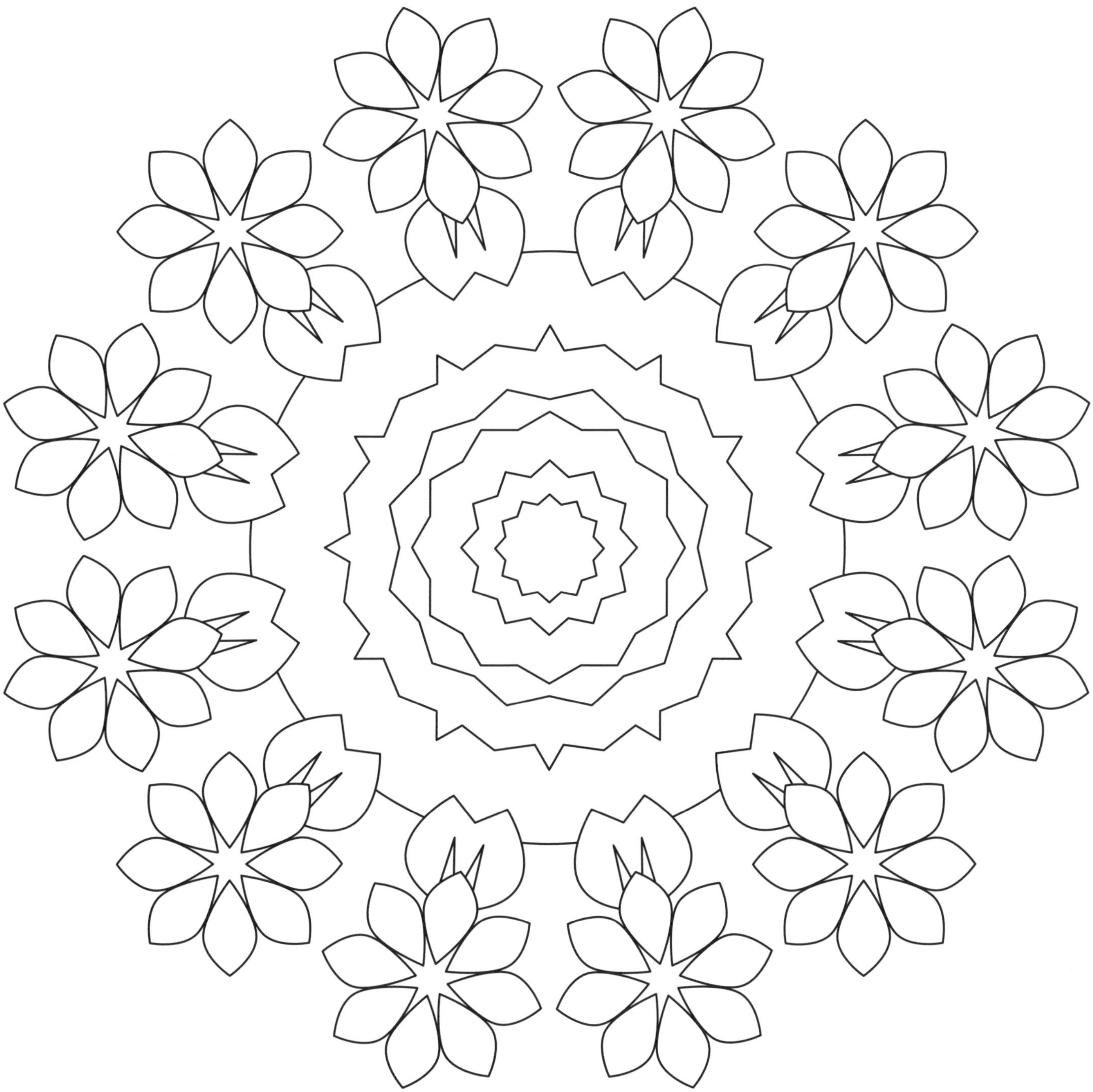

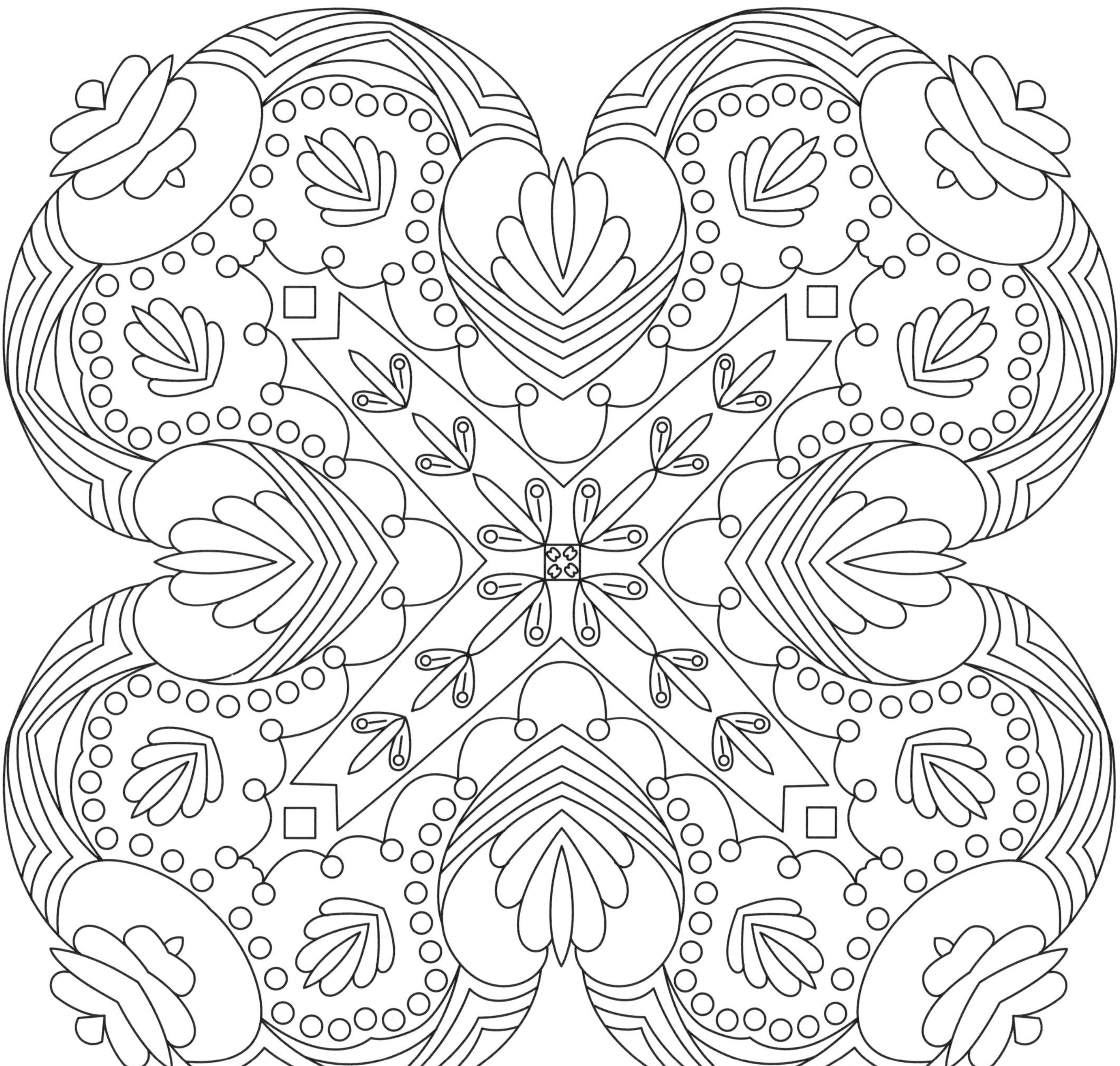

About the Author...Linda M. Poole

When I was a little girl, I had an insatiable desire to make things. Luckily, I come from a family that understood me all too well. My roots have been firmly planted by a talented, loving, generous European family that always put family first and strongly encouraged freedom of artistic expression. I have inherited the good fortune of learning from generations of artists, silversmiths, sculptors, poets, weavers, stained glass artisans, and writers.

My maternal grandmother let me work the treadle part of the sewing machine while she sewed. My grandmother was a smart cookie. She found a way of giving an energetic little girl a way to have fun and participate. Soon, she propped me on her lap and showed me how to sew.

I had my own needles, scissors, and threads before kindergarten and was taught to respect my tools. I remember my mother teaching me to crochet, knit, and embroider. My father took me on adventures. I always had my little Instamatic camera in tow. My Christmas gifts were always about art, sewing, and creating. An artist's easel, paints, brushes, paper, and my own art table were some of my favorite gifts. As an adult looking back, I am thankful for the thought and time my parents gave to nurturing my curiosity and love for art.

My whole life has always revolved around photography, writing, painting, and sewing. These interests have fueled my passion for travel, teaching, and sharing my experiences with people around the world. I have taught throughout the United States, the United Kingdom, Germany, Turkey, and Italy. I believe language is never a barrier in the translation of quilts or art.

Linda Poole lives with her husband, Ray Williams, and Corgi pup, Zoie, near Milford, Pennsylvania, a beautiful region in the northeastern part of the state. Together they share the passion of discovering the gifts of nature while hiking trails that lead to creeks, brooks, rivers, and lakes. Ray can be found with his fishing pole in hand with Linda by his side, clicking away with her camera.

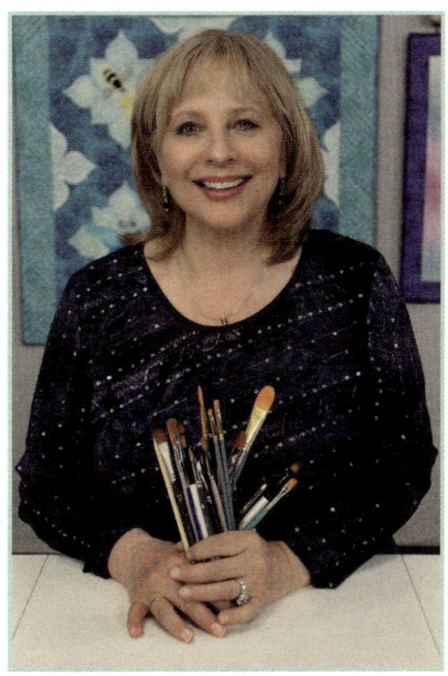